Guerrilla Marketing

Online Weapons

Other Books by Jay Conrad Levinson

The Most Important $1.00 Book Ever Written

Secrets of Successful Free-Lancing

San Francisco: An Unusual Guide to Unusual Shopping
   (with Pat Levinson and John Bear)

Earning Money Without a Job

555 Ways to Earn Extra Money

150 Secrets of Successful Weight Loss
   (with Michael Levin and Michael Rokeach, M.D.)

Quit Your Job!

An Earthling's Guide to Satellite TV

Guerrilla Marketing

Guerrilla Marketing Attack

Guerrilla Marketing Weapons

The 90-Minute Hour

Guerrilla Financing
   (with Bruce Jan Blechman)

Guerrilla Selling
   (with Bill Gallagher and Orvel Ray Wilson)

Guerrilla Marketing Excellence

Guerrilla Advertising

Guerrilla Marketing Online
   (with Charles Rubin)

Other Books by Charles Rubin

Thinking Small: The Buyer's Guide to Portable Computers

The Endless Apple

AppleWorks: Boosting Your Business with Integrated Software

Command Performance: AppleWorks

Microsoft Works on the Apple Macintosh

Macintosh Hard Disk Management

Running Microsoft Works

The Macintosh Bible "What Do I Do Now?" Book

The Macintosh Bible Guide to System 7

The Macintosh Bible Guide to FileMaker Pro 3.0

The Macintosh Bible Guide to System 7.1

The Macintosh Bible Guide to ClarisWorks 4.0

The Little Book of Computer Wisdom: How to Make Friends
with Your PC or Mac

Guerrilla Marketing Online
(with Jay Conrad Levinson)

Guerrilla Marketing Online Weapons

100 Low-Cost, High-Impact Weapons

for Online Profits and Prosperity

Jay Conrad Levinson

and **Charles Rubin**

HOUGHTON MIFFLIN COMPANY

Boston   New York

For information about permission to reproduce selections from this book,
write to Permissions, Houghton Mifflin Company, 215 Park Avenue South,
New York, New York 10003.

For information about this and other Houghton Mifflin trade and
reference books and multimedia products, visit The Bookstore at
Houghton Mifflin on the World Wide Web at http://www.hmco.com/trade/.

Library of Congress Cataloging-in-Publication Data
Levinson, Jay Conrad.
Guerrilla marketing online weapons / Jay Conrad Levinson and Charles Rubin.
    p.   cm.
  ISBN 0-395-77019-X
  1. Internet marketing.   2. Internet advertising.   I. Rubin, Charles, 1953–
II. Title.
HF4515.1265.L48   1996
658.8'00285'467 — dc20   96-10875   CIP

Printed in the United States of America
MP 10 9 8 7 6 5 4

This book is dedicated to Ron Lichty and Michael Rogers, who steered me toward cyberspace many years ago. I hope the ride has been half as much fun for you as it has for me.

— C.R.

This book is also dedicated to Neil Quateman, Robert Pope, Bill Gallagher Jr., Christine Sizemore, Fran Syufy, and Deborah Brockman, my supernovas in cyberspace. May your stars shine as brightly.

— J.C.L.

Contents

Introduction

WHEN WE WROTE *Guerrilla Marketing Online* in 1994, the business community was just waking up to the potential of online marketing. As we write this in 1995, the rush to do business on the Internet is in high gear. More than 85 percent of the networks connected to the online world are now commercial. Every month, another 10,000 commercial networks are registered on the Net. And with the networks come individual users, as many as 500,000 new ones every month. To put it briefly, fellow guerrillas, *it's a jungle out there!*

As in any jungle, there are those who strike it rich, those who make plans and fail, and those who simply wander around lost, without a clue. The winners understand the unique qualities of the online market and the special needs of their online customers. The winners are marketing guerrillas who use their time, energy, and imagination to outmaneuver their competitors in cyberspace. It takes guts, attitude, and determination to succeed, but the size of your business or your marketing budget has nothing to do with it.

ONLINE BATTLEGROUNDS

In *Guerrilla Marketing Online*, we outlined the basic characteristics of the online marketplace and looked at major battlegrounds, targets, and tactics for success. Among the battlegrounds we covered were:

> *electronic mail*, the Internet's messaging system;
> *online storefronts*, where companies, individuals, and organizations present information about their products or services;
> *online advertising* via classified ad areas, Worldwide Web billboards, bulletin board systems, and Net directories where customers can locate your business;

discussion groups, where communities of Net users meet to talk about specific topics;

conferences in forums on online services and on bulletin board systems, where you can demonstrate your know-how for an online audience; and

electronic publishing, which lets you establish your expertise and credibility by placing tip sheets, articles, and other publications in various locations throughout cyberspace.

Each of these battlegrounds represents a means to potential profits, but success isn't automatic. The Net is no more an instant key to riches than television or radio is. Many companies have stumbled badly in the online marketplace, spending thousands of dollars for minuscule results. Guerrillas tackle cyberspace with a head start, because they know that success depends not on the Net itself but on the strategy and weapons they use in attacking it.

THREE STEPS TO ONLINE SUCCESS

In this book, we'll look closely at one hundred specific weapons you can use to succeed in cyberspace. All these weapons support the three key strategies that ensure online success.

1. Seek online visibility. Cyberspace is dark and crowded, and visibility is hard to achieve. Putting up a Web page isn't enough. Promote your business by:

announcing it in classified ads;

participating in discussion groups related to your business;

publishing documents or holding online conferences that showcase your expertise;

placing listings in online directories, sponsorship notices, and Worldwide Web billboards; and

providing information about your business and your area of expertise in a storefront.

Promotion doesn't mean broadcasting an ad in every possible location in the online market — that can actually do you more harm than good. For a guerrilla, promotion means finding out each of the destinations on the infobahn where your customers congregate or visit and then learning how to place your company name and key messages before those customers in a way appropriate to each location.

2. Build online credibility. Everyone is equal in cyberspace. It's hard to tell the winners from the losers with just a glance, and you have to find ways to distinguish yourself as one of the good guys. You must establish credibility with your prospects before you can hope to do business.

As you distribute appropriate messages about your business in places where your customers are likely to see them, pack as much useful, noncommercial information into them as possible. Use the Net's cheap, effective communications facilities to demonstrate your expertise, reliability, and professionalism, rather than simply placing ads for your business. And don't think you'll constantly have to churn out new insights: you can use your computer's storage, editing, and retrieval capabilities to recycle and reformat information. One good tip sheet or article can serve a dozen different needs if you manipulate it properly.

The more information you provide and the more useful it is to your prospective customers, the better your online credibility will be. Quality information equals credibility, and credibility equals customers.

3. Nurture online relationships. Cyberspace is an anonymous place, and customers are wary about buying from people they don't know. Establish personal relationships to overcome the Net's anonymity and build trust. As people begin placing orders, requesting proposals, or asking you for further information about your business, nurture these relationships with personalized attention, superior service, and timely follow-ups.

For example, address each customer as an individual. You probably have a prewritten electronic brochure you mail out to prospects, but a would-be buyer will feel more at home if you send it out with a personal greeting. A single introductory sentence preceding your electronic brochure can turn an anonymous response into the beginning of a real relationship.

WHY A BOOK OF WEAPONS?

Knowing the basic elements of success isn't the same as conducting a successful attack. In *Guerrilla Marketing Online*, we went into great detail about each of the steps involved in a guerrilla attack and briefly touched on seventy-five online marketing weapons you can use to conduct it. In this book, we'll focus on a hundred specific weapons that will ensure your success.

We focus on weapons here because individually, the weapons are easy to understand, easy to implement, and easy to track. There are dozens of opportunities for marketing online, hundreds of places in which to do it, and an ever-changing environment in which it all takes place. For most people (including small business owners who don't surf the Net for a living), the sheer number of options for online marketing can seem overwhelming.

But once you understand the keys to success, you can continually improve your attack by thinking about which weapons you're using, learning how to use those weapons better, and adding new ones as you go along. Most of the weapons covered in this book cost nothing but your time. Most of them aren't being used and aren't even understood by your competitors. The more weapons you use, the more successful you'll be. You may never get to the point where you're using all one hundred weapons (and even if you do, new ones are appearing constantly), but by striving to use as many as possible, you'll be able to stay well ahead of the competition.

THERE'S NO SUBSTITUTE FOR EFFORT

Online marketing involves computers, but it's not a magic shortcut to profits. The Internet isn't an automated marketing machine that does your job for you; it's just a remarkably efficient and inexpensive communications medium. You can use the Net to reach customers around the world or to target a specific group of prospects by their area of interest, but the Net won't do the work for you. Each of the weapons in this book involves at least some effort. Fortunately, your efforts will be well rewarded.

The Net can also be a two-edged sword. Use a weapon well, and it adds to your prestige and profits. Use it badly, and it has the opposite effect. As a friend of ours likes to say, "Good advertising helps a bad product fail more quickly." The Net is a turbo-charged medium where reputations can be made or broken at the speed of light.

If understanding a weapon were the only key to success, then everyone who read this book would be an online marketing hero. But knowing what a weapon is and using it are two different things. Like marketing success anywhere, online marketing success requires planning, dedication, guts, and a commitment of time and energy. Understanding that you'll need to commit time and budget for it is one of the weapons we'll discuss in Chapter 2.

WHAT MAKES A WEAPON?

In guerrilla terms, a marketing weapon is anything you use to improve your communications or relations with customers, lower your cost of doing business, or increase your profits. In short, it's any method you use to gain a competitive edge. That's a pretty broad definition, but we've divided the book into fourteen chapters to organize weapons into different categories. Let's take a look.

Your business mission
In Chapter 1, we'll look at five weapons that relate to your business mission. Having a business mission means identifying a unique niche for your business, a specific online goal you want to reach, and a strategy for reaching it. If your business doesn't have a specific mission, you'll have a lot of trouble identifying and achieving your goals.

Planning and organization
Getting a piece of information from the Net is like getting a drink of water from a fire hose. Whenever you're online, so much information is coming at you from all directions that your attack can be derailed by the torrent of distractions. You need to plan your attack in advance, execute it faithfully, and be very well organized as you proceed. Chapter 2 offers six weapons you can use to stay focused.

Presence

Cyberspace is a big dark room where thousands of businesses compete for customers' attention. Your online presence defines you and your company — it is a unique identity that separates you from your competitors. You must carefully build and consistently maintain your presence if you want to attract your share of online profits. Chapter 3 offers ten weapons you can use to create and maintain an online presence.

Service

The online marketplace has huge potential, but you won't maximize it for your own profits unless you deliver superior service. Given the choice, your customers would rather buy from a human being than a computer. The nine service-related weapons in Chapter 4 will give customers some compelling reasons to do business with you online.

Customer comfort

People have an inherent distrust of computers. As the Net extends the reach of computer users around the world, it also magnifies a typical customer's technophobia. (TV and newspaper reports of crime and pornography on the Net don't help, either.) Your marketing efforts should include an array of weapons that ease customers' distrust and make them feel safe. Use the nine weapons in Chapter 5 to build your own customer comfort zone.

Advertising

Advertising is a key component of any marketing campaign, and it's doubly important in the darkness of cyberspace. Thousands of companies clamor for attention on the Net, and advertising helps you gain your share of prospective customers' attention. In Chapter 6, we'll look at eleven weapons you can use to advertise your online business.

Publicity

Publicity is another key component of a good marketing campaign. Many of your customers will learn about your online business by reading about it in a print or online publication. Use the seven weapons in Chapter 7 to publicize your online efforts.

Goodwill
Goodwill refers to the good relationships you have with customers and suppliers, and it's a big part of your online identity. Off-line, companies sponsor cultural events, donate goods or services, and find other ways to build a positive identity in their communities. With the Net's communications magic, your efforts at public service and community involvement can boost your reputation around the world. Chapter 8 presents seven weapons you can use to make this happen.

Free information
You deliver free information constantly in your off-line marketing efforts by simply answering questions, posting signs in your store, and offering brochures. When you don't have a physical presence, free information becomes a crucial method of demonstrating your expertise and professionalism to others. In Chapter 9, we'll look at twelve weapons you can use to distribute free information and enhance your online reputation.

Giveaways
Everyone gives away information on the Net, but offering other freebies makes your company more attractive to the casual Net surfer. Free merchandise, services, and special discounts are proven ways of drawing crowds to your online storefront or e-mail box. Chapter 10 offers five weapons you can use to attract attention with giveaways.

Special events
Special events are another way to rise above the noise level in cyberspace. Contests, grand openings, seminars, and celebrity appearances are all weapons you can use to gain free visibility and generate excitement about your online efforts. See Chapter 11 for more on these weapons.

Referrals
Satisfied customers are the best source of new business, and the Net makes it easy for your customers to spread the word about your

products or services. In Chapter 12, we'll look at four ways to use customer referrals to build sales and profits.

Intelligence

The online world is a vast storehouse of information you can use to spot buying trends, learn more about your competitors, and get expert advice on a variety of topics. The more you know about this world, the better you'll understand how to profit from it. In Chapter 13, we'll look at four specific weapons you can use to deepen your understanding of the online market.

Guerrilla attitudes

Your guerrilla attitudes affect everything you do as an online marketer. In Chapter 14, you'll discover seven weapons that enable you to approach the online market like a true guerrilla.

HOW TO USE THIS BOOK

The goal of every guerrilla is to use as many marketing weapons as possible. If you're brand-new to the online market, get an online account and poke around until you understand e-mail, discussions, and the Worldwide Web. Pick up a copy of *Guerrilla Marketing Online* to get a general orientation to approaching these marketing battlegrounds and developing an online marketing plan. Once you're familiar with the terrain, you're ready to put this book to work.

To start with, go through the book from front to back and make two lists: one containing the names of all the online marketing weapons you think you're using right now (or plan to use first if you're not online yet), and one with the names of weapons you're not using now and don't plan to use later. If you come across a term you don't recognize, check the glossary at the back of the book for a definition. You'll find that the weapons are covered roughly in order, from those you need at the beginning of your attack or before it begins to those you'll use after the attack is under way.

Next, read about the weapons you're using now or plan to use first. If you're already online, think about how you can use each of those weapons better. Remember, a weapon badly used can do you more harm than a weapon not used at all. For example, a poorly designed e-mail signature can turn customers away just as easily as a well-designed signature can bring them in (see p. 23 in Chapter 3).

Once your existing weapons are honed to perfection, go through the list of weapons you're not using now and make plans to use as many of them as possible. Most of the weapons in this book cost nothing more than your time, yet our experience shows that most of the people doing business online today are using fewer than twenty of them. Each new weapon you use — or each existing weapon you use more effectively — increases your chances of success. Make it your goal to use at least fifty of the weapons offered here.

KEEPING SCORE

This book is a manual for success. Working with one weapon at a time, you can create an effective attack and improve it as you go along. Using these weapons makes your efforts manageable, and you get better results with each new one you bring into battle.

The online marketplace is still very young. The biggest successes have yet to happen; the most lucrative battles have yet to be fought. Approach your online marketing attack one weapon at a time and constantly strive to do better. With the weapons in this book and the determination to use them, you can defeat your competitors in cyberspace and reap the spoils of victory.

Your Business Mission

IF THE INTERNET marketplace were a city, it would look a lot like New York City at rush hour, and everyone would be blindfolded. Most of the companies and individuals rushing to market themselves online have no specific goals, no specific plan, and no method of measuring their success. Rather than thinking about why they're going online, what they hope to achieve there, and how an online presence can add value to their business from the customer's point of view, most of today's online marketers are clambering onto the Net bandwagon because it seems like the right thing to do.

Guerrillas know better. Going on the Net might be the right thing to do, but your attack must be designed, planned, and executed specifically for the special demands of cyberspace. The online market is crowded and noisy. Your business must have a unique identity that instantly lifts it above the noise level and fixes it in the minds of your customers.

In this chapter, we'll look at five weapons that you can use before you ever go online to make your business a standout when you do. None of these weapons costs anything but your time and imagination, but all of them are critical to your long-term success.

1 PRODUCT/SERVICE NICHE

Your niche is your particular position in the marketplace and in the customer's mind. It's what makes your business stand out from others. One way to stand out is to offer a product or service that's difficult or impossible to get elsewhere, but uniqueness can be hard to come by in a global marketplace like the Net. If you're thinking you'll have the only flower shop on the Net, for example, you'll find that lots of other flower sellers have already gone online.

Another way to stand out is to offer better quality, faster service, more expertise, higher credibility, or a more personal touch. All these attributes can become part of your business identity.

When thinking about your niche, don't kid yourself into believing that simply taking your business online makes you unique. The online marketplace doesn't change your product; it just changes the way you market it. Even if you happen to be the first company to offer a particular product or service on the Net, you won't be the only one for long.

But don't be discouraged to find you have competitors. Competition means you're not the only one who sees an opening — it verifies your hunch that you're on to a profitable opportunity. Guerrillas thrive on competition, because they can use their energy and imagination to outmaneuver it. The challenge is to stake out your own piece of terrain in your business area and defend it with everything you've got. Here's how.

Before you leap into cyberspace, survey the competition in your business area and look for unfilled niches, or for niches that you can fill better. What begin as large holes in the marketplace become a series of smaller holes filled by individual products or businesses. For example, there's a growing demand for companies that help publicize businesses on the Net. The first company in this business attracted clients from all manner of industries. But servicing such a diversified clientele is really too large a niche for just one company to fill adequately — there are too many publicity outlets in cyberspace and too many companies trying to exploit them.

Now there are opportunities to carve out particular niches within the general marketplace for Internet publicity services. One company might specialize in publicity on the commercial online services, while a second specializes in promoting via bulletin board systems. One firm might specialize in promoting books and authors, while another promotes legal or accounting firms. Very often, a niche that represents an opportunity for more than one business can be subdivided into two or more unique niches.

To develop a niche for your business, ask yourself the following questions.

Why is your business successful now? What quality (selection, service, price, expertise, etc.) makes people do business with you instead of your competition?

Can you fill the same niche in cyberspace? Think about whether the competitive advantages you enjoy off-line will work for you online; sometimes they won't. If your furniture store's reputation in a geographical area or its physical location are major factors in your success, for example, you'll have to find a different advantage when you go online.

If possible, choose an online niche that leverages the powers of the Net. For instance, your furniture store's online niche might be a catalog and design service that allows customers to view dozens of sofas in different colors or easily compare the dimensions and seating capacity of dining room sets. This kind of instant comparison shopping is impossible to achieve outside cyberspace.

Survey your online competitors by searching the Worldwide Web or browsing among newsgroups and classified ad areas, and determine which niches they're filling. You'll probably find that most of them haven't identified a specific niche. By staking out a niche for yourself, you'll be on the way to a unique business identity.

Can you defend your position in this niche against all competitors? What appears to be a unique niche today may not be one tomorrow. Rather than choosing a niche such as "the only [fill in the blank] business in cyberspace," look for a more specific advantage that your company clearly has and can maintain.

Of the advantages you might choose, service, quality, specialization, and expertise are some of the easiest to claim and defend. Price and breadth of selection are more vulnerable to attack, because any larger, better-financed competitor can outmaneuver you in these areas. Hang your reputation on your selection of 10,000 sports trading cards, for example, and your business could be hung when someone comes along with 50,000 cards. On the other hand, personal service and a unique selection of antique trading cards are niches that are much more difficult to challenge.

Think carefully about the niche you want to occupy in cyberspace. It may be slightly different from the one you occupy off-line, but that's all right, as long as you can successfully promote and defend it. Once you've defined a unique niche for your company, make sure all your marketing efforts reflect your ownership of it. The other weapons in this chapter will help you do that.

Note: For a masterly explanation of market niches and how to select and defend them, we highly recommend the book *Positioning*, by Al Ries and Jack Trout (New York: Warner, 1987).

2   MISSION STATEMENT

Your mission statement specifies your reason for being in business, your goal in being online, and your method of reaching that goal, all rolled up in a sentence or two. Most of the companies that fail in the online marketplace do so because they haven't identified a specific mission. Large companies can afford to put up Worldwide Web sites or storefronts on online services as trial balloons, just for the experience. Small businesses can't afford to drift aimlessly on the Net in the hope of finding a profitable destination. If you don't know where you're going, you don't have much chance of getting there. By identifying your mission and periodically reviewing it, you'll have a specific goal to work toward, a means of keeping your marketing attack focused, and a way to measure your progress.

Make your business mission as specific as possible. It's not good enough to say that your mission is to improve sales or make money. Your mission statement should specify not only the goal but how you plan to reach it. Your statement should also be plain enough for anyone in your company to understand. Let's look at two examples.

> *Infotime Research will develop an international market by offering superior customer service with a Web site that allows online patent, trademark, and licensing searches.*

In one sentence, this company identifies its niche (superior customer service), its method of filling that niche on the Net (a Web site that allows online searches), and its customer base (an international market of people performing patent, trademark, and licensing searches).

> *InstaPix will expand its national market, improve customer service, and cut shipping costs with an online catalog that delivers professional-quality image files to graphic artists within minutes.*

This mission statement identifies three goals (an expanded national market, improved customer service, and lower shipping costs), a method of reaching them (an online catalog), and a target market (graphic artists). InstaPix's chosen niches have to do with service and convenience.

Notice, too, that part of InstaPix's mission is to save money by using the Net as a distribution system. Guerrillas seek any advantage they can get over their competitors, and saving money by electronic distribution means there's more money available for marketing, research, and other weapons. In fact, your online mission might be primarily to lower distribution or marketing costs rather than make sales or attract new business. Companies like Adobe Systems, Sun Microsystems, and Silicon Graphics save hundreds of thousands of dollars a year by distributing software or sales literature electronically instead of through conventional mail.

Whatever your mission, it should be straightforward enough so you can summarize it in a short, simple statement like the ones above.

3   BUSINESS NAME

Without the benefit of a physical storefront or your personal physical presence, a business name takes on much more importance in cyberspace. If you use the business name in your e-mail address or as your network domain name, it becomes the first thing people see when you send them e-mail or post a message to a discussion group on the Net. A clever, evocative name in the From box of an e-mail message can start your marketing campaign on the right foot.

If you have an existing off-line business that you want to expand into cyberspace, you'll naturally want to use the same business name. But if you're going into business from scratch, you have the opportunity to choose a name that makes a significant contribution to your marketing attack.

Your name should accomplish the following tasks.

It should describe your business without limiting possible future expansion. For example, *Ace Mystery Books* is very descriptive, but it will be a problem if you later want to expand into cookbooks.

It should be easy to spell. Most communication on the Net is written. Don't choose a name that makes it harder for prospects or customers to communicate with you. Keep it short, if possible. Avoid using *z*'s, *x*'s, or numbers in the name — most people have more trouble typing these characters accurately than any others. If you're using an existing business name that's long and complex, come up with a shorter version of it for your e-mail user name or network domain name. For example, instead of using *guerrillamarketing.com*, we use *gmarketing.com*. Generally, the shorter your online address, the less chance that people will mistype it and fail to reach you.

It should be unusual enough so it's not easily confused with another name. Major corporations spend thousands of dollars on consultants to dream up names like Aptiva, Navistar, and Unisys, but you can distinguish your company name in other ways. Advertising agencies, law firms, accounting firms, and architects often use their partners' names to identify themselves, because each collection of names is unique. Besides, a string of partner names sounds more professional than something like *Ace Advertising*, *Acme Architects*, or *Able Accounting*.

Your name followed by & *Associates* is likely to be unique and is general enough to accommodate any business venture you might want to expand into later on. You can even add a descriptive word or two to identify your business at the same time, as with *Alvey Marketing Associates* or *Fernandez Environmental Engineers*.

Many new cyberspace firms make the mistake of including *Internet* or *Electronic* in their business names. The trouble is that many of these names sound alike, and the Net abounds with them. It gets difficult after a while to tell names like *Electronic Marketing Associates*, *Internet Marketing Associates*, *The Internet Company*, *Internet Presence, Inc.*, and so on apart. Rather than helping your business to have its own identity, such names reinforce the Net's anonymity. In the resulting confusion, your prospect may end up contacting a competing firm with a similar name rather than yours. However, we've also seen names that describe a Net-related business well, such as *NetPost*, the name of a firm that handles Internet publicity.

It shouldn't have any negative connotations. Refer back to your niche and mission statement and make sure your name doesn't work against your identity in the niche you've claimed. For example,

Value and *Rapid* have good connotations; *Cheap* and *Rush* can have bad ones. And don't forget you're on the Net: avoid names that have secondary meanings in cyberspace. Tempting as it might be, for example, *spam.com* might not be the best domain name for the Hormel Company; in cyberspace, to *spam* is to distribute junk e-mail or newsgroup messages indiscriminately.

It shouldn't be so cute or trendy that your customers won't understand it. Like other subcultures, cyberspace has its own heroes, villains, and buzzwords. But many of the people joining the online market these days are just regular consumers who aren't steeped in the traditions of techno-life. If you sell computer services, you might name your company after a Unix command or a minor character in *Star Trek*, or after a lesser-known Net service like Ping or Whois, but such names will be meaningless or confusing to nontechnical consumers.

It should be easy to find. Finally, remember that your name will compete with dozens or hundreds of others in Internet lists or directories. If your online attack relies heavily on listings in online directories or on being easy to locate with one of the Net's search engines, choose a name that begins with A, so anyone searching the Net or browsing through a directory will come across it before the name of any potential competitors. This is a tried-and-true technique from telephone book advertising that still pays off, even though most prospects are on to it.

A business name is as important in cyberspace as it is in the off-line world. Keep these criteria in mind and choose yours carefully.

4   THEME

A theme is a short phrase or slogan that crystallizes your business identity and becomes by itself as memorable as a brand name. You can use a theme in your e-mail or discussion group signature, on your Worldwide Web home page, and as a tag line on every electronic document you publish or transmit. A good theme is hard to find, but if you can come up with one, it will help establish and maintain your online presence.

The best themes identify a company's position, the place it hopes to occupy among its competitors in the prospect's mind. They also accomplish this goal in half a dozen words or less. Here are some great examples:

> *Fly the friendly skies of United*
> *We try harder*
> *We bring good things to light*
> *All the news that's fit to print*

Although the actual company name is included in only the first of these themes, we recognize the others instantly as representing (respectively) Avis Rent A Car, General Electric, and the *New York Times.* Ideally, your theme should fit your company so perfectly that it doesn't need to include your company name — the theme instantly identifies your company in the customer's mind.

The best way to come up with a theme is to consider your unique niche and then think of a way to express that in a few words. Decide what the single most important aspect of your business is (service, selection, convenience, quality, expertise, etc.) and find a way to express it as a theme. If necessary, survey your customers and ask them to come up with the one word or the one reason that they do business with you. Think about what brings you business and then figure out how to express that as a theme.

For example, Avis knew it was second to Hertz in the auto rental business, but it used that as an advantage, with a theme that expresses a stronger desire to deliver service. It's possible to imagine that Avis's theme came from a customer focus group where a customer said, "They try harder," when asked why he or she chose Avis instead of Hertz.

Another way to develop a theme is to look at a good list of power words and think about the ones that fit in with your business mission. Words like *value, safe, proven, results,* and *good* all cause positive reactions when people hear or see them. Having one or more power words in a theme will get you on the right track.

A good theme will help you rise above the noise level of the Net by spelling out what your company stands for in one simple phrase. It gives your business extra differentiation from the thousands of other businesses online.

5 IDENTITY

Your business identity is the sum of your unique business characteristics. Just like an individual's personality, a business's identity is one of a kind and honest. While the realities of cyberspace make it easy for a business to project a certain *image*, a façade intended to create an impression, your customers will eventually see through it if it is false. When you're just projecting an image, you're playing a role: you behave one way for one customer in one situation and another way for another customer in another situation. The trouble with such an image is that it's not really you, and eventually you'll have trouble remembering which façade you presented when. Therefore, your business image should also be your true identity.

If everything you do on the Net reflects your true business identity, there's no façade to fall apart. You can conduct all your business exactly as your business values dictate. By doing all your business in a manner consistent with your real identity, you never have to worry about contradicting something you said or did before. If you're honest and straightforward in all your dealings, your customers will quickly realize that what they see is the real thing.

To discover your true business identity, sit down with a few key employees and perhaps a few key customers or business associates and list some words or phrases that really define your company. If you're aware of having tried to present an image in the past, try contrasting the identity words or phrases with image words or phrases, so everyone in your company understands the difference between the real identity and the false image.

For example, an online travel agency going through this exercise might come up with lists like this:

Image	Identity
Lowest prices	Competitive prices
Experts in everything	Alaska/Mexico cruise experts
Worldwide service	Small but personalized

Once you've come up with some words that define your business accurately, reflect your identity in all your business operations, from the copy in your ads and brochures to the way your employees interact with customers and suppliers. Your identity can be reflected in your business mission statement, your theme, your e-mail signature, and even in the name of your company, your products, or your services.

If you work hard to convey your true identity in everything you do, you'll find it much easier to establish a unique presence from which you can profit on the Internet.

2

Planning and Organization

"SO MUCH TO DO, so little time" is the entrepreneur's constant refrain. But you haven't seen anything until you've been on the Net. So much information comes at you online that the time you spend there becomes very precious. Your ability to capture and organize the information you receive and deal with it effectively can make or break your marketing attack.

With so much happening, it's also easy to become distracted. You may start out wanting to monitor a couple of online discussions, for example, but then go off in search of new Web sites or other re-sources mentioned in those discussions. And if the resources you find are interesting enough, you might forget all about your original intention to participate in a discussion group.

A solid plan and the discipline to follow it are your only defense against the Net's inevitable distractions. Even when you're not dis-tracted, a plan lets you make the best use of your time. There are hundreds of places to market online, but your attack plan will direct you to the most promising ones. It takes into account your resources and goals, your competition, and your customers; it's your road map to success.

In this chapter, we'll look at six weapons you can use to plan and organize your marketing attack.

6 AN ONLINE MARKETING PLAN

Your online marketing plan is a blueprint that spells out what you hope to accomplish and how you'll accomplish it. It starts with your mission statement (see p. 4 in Chapter 1), but then it focuses your energies by identifying specific resources, battle targets, and weap-ons you'll use to reach your goal.

A good marketing plan should be brief and tightly focused. Large companies often develop lengthy marketing plans that seem designed to impress corporate executives with their weight and thickness. But long-winded plans are often so confusing or intimidating that they're never properly implemented. Guerrillas take action, so your marketing plan should be something you and your staff can easily understand and put to work immediately.

In addition to the goal you identified in your mission statement, the key elements of your marketing plan are your resources, targets, and weapons. As we'll see, your resources budget helps you determine which targets to attack, and the targets determine which weapons you'll need.

Resources. Your online attack will never get off the ground unless you have the time, personnel, and money to implement it, so your first task is to prepare a budget for it.

The most important resource you'll devote to online marketing is time. It takes time to check and respond to your electronic mail, time to design, implement, and maintain an electronic storefront, time to monitor and participate in online discussions, and so on. You can have the greatest intentions in the world, but they won't amount to anything if you don't have the time to execute them.

In preparing your plan, think about how many minutes or hours per day or per week you and your staff can devote to online marketing. Come up with a realistic figure that allows you to integrate online marketing with the rest of your daily activities. Many people set aside a quarter- or half-hour at a particular time of day, perhaps just before lunch, for their online marketing tasks.

Once you've chosen a time budget, let it determine the scope of your attack. It's better to choose targets based on the amount of time you have than to choose the targets first and hope you'll have time to attack them properly. Besides, you'll probably want to roll your plan out gradually. Unless you're a cyberspace regular, it's better to begin your attack with a wholehearted effort on one front than to attack weakly on three or four different fronts.

Don't assume you'll "find the time" in between all the other things you're doing right now — you won't. Instead, come up with a specific time budget and figure out exactly when you'll allocate that time during your day. For example, checking your e-mail and responding to it will probably take five or ten minutes a day in the beginning. Set your computer to check your e-mail box automatically at certain times of the day, and decide on a specific time to read and respond to new mail. Your goal should be to answer every piece of e-mail within one business day. Allow enough time to prepare and mail responses promptly.

If you have a staff, you can probably divide up the online marketing duties among several people. Maybe one person can check your company's e-mail box and then route appropriate messages to different employees for follow-up. Maybe you'll assign one person to participate in one discussion group while a second person participates in another. By spreading the load around, you can minimize the time costs for any one person, yet sustain an attack on several targets at once.

Along with the time costs you'll have to consider your money budget. Costs include setup and monthly access charges for an online account; classified advertising fees; storefront design, setup, and maintenance fees; training and staff salaries for the attack; computer equipment; and telephone line charges. Decide how much you can spend to get the attack rolling and how much you're willing to put up to maintain it month after month.

Targets. After you've decided how much time you and your staff can spend online, choose the targets for your attack. In *Guerrilla Marketing Online,* we identified several types of targets:

- discussion groups
- electronic storefronts
- advertising locations
- conference venues
- electronic publishing locations.

Each target requires a specific time commitment, so the number of targets you choose will be determined by your time budget. At the beginning, though, it's better to attack several targets of the same type than to choose a variety of targets. For example, rather than mixing a discussion group, a storefront, a classified advertising campaign, and an electronic publishing schedule in your plan, focus on one of these areas and pursue the attack there. Once you're comfortable with that aspect of your attack and it's a normal part of your day, expand the attack into other areas. Each kind of target has its own requirements and tactics, and it's better to learn one method of attack really well before moving into others.

Weapons. Weapons are the tools you'll need to attack each of your primary targets. Dozens of weapons are discussed in this book, and you'll use many of them in your online battles. Your online marketing plan should specify which weapons you need for your attack. Here's a list of targets and some weapons associated with each of them:

Discussion groups — one or more signatures, an electronic brochure, canned messages, a mailbot

Electronic storefronts — a storefront design, a logo, graphics, text, a storefront location, a domain name, and a plan for how the store's contents will evolve over time

Advertising — ad subject lines, ad copy, a billboard design, ad locations, a follow-up message, an ad monitoring and response tracking system

Conferences — a conference pitch, a preconference information sheet about you and your business, and a list of suggested questions

Electronic publishing — a plan for publishing a series of documents in a particular location, the electronic documents themselves, a signature or introductory paragraph that identifies you and your business and how to get further information, and a system to track what you published, where, and when.

Here's a plan for a small T-shirt printing company that wants to expand into the online marketplace.

Mission statement: The Club T-Shirt Company will develop a market for specialty shirts in online clubs and organizations by building visibility and credibility in targeted discussion groups.

Resources: Startup time — 5 hours. Maintenance time — $1/2$ man/ hour per day. Startup cost — $100 for modem. Maintenance cost — $50/month for accounts on four major online services.

Targets: Hobby-oriented discussion groups on CompuServe, Prodigy, and America Online, such as America Online's Aviation Forum.

Weapons: Classified ads, discussion group participation, e-mail letter to forum administrators, signature, follow-up message, electronic brochure.

This attack can easily be carried out by one or two people, is very inexpensive to start and maintain, and can later be expanded with a storefront or electronic catalog as business and the number of target markets grow.

7 MARCHING ORDERS

Marching orders are specific tasks you'll carry out to maintain your attack each day, week, month, or quarter. A list of marching orders is your lifeline in the turbulent seas of cyberspace, because it keeps you focused on carrying out your key marketing tasks every day. Your list of marching orders should arise naturally out of your online marketing plan.

Once you have a list of orders, it's much easier to stay focused on the tasks you need to do. Here's an example based on the Club T-Shirt Company marketing plan outlined above.

Daily tasks: Check e-mail, check classified ad position, monitor discussion groups and respond as necessary.

Weekly tasks: Evaluate ad responses, scout new ad locations.

Monthly tasks: Expand attack into a new discussion group.

Quarterly tasks: Conduct seasonal promotion, distribute new sales letter to forum and discussion group administrators.

8 AN ACTIVITY LOG

Unless you have an extremely simple marketing attack, you'll need an activity log to keep track of your targets, battles, and weapons. It's easy to forget what you did last, where and when you uploaded an electronic publication, or when you last posted a discussion group message. An activity log will help you remember what you did and when you did it.

Activity logs are particularly important for tracking classified ads, discussion group announcements, storefront changes, and electronic publications. You can create a log simply by recording each day's activities with a word-processing program, or you can use a simple database program to create individual records that track your activity in various parts of cyberspace. You can even keep track of your online activities on a piece of paper.

You'll want to keep information like this:

Start date — The date you first posted a message, uploaded a file to a library, opened a storefront, or began participating in a discussion

Latest date — The last time you modified a store, reposted an ad, contributed to a discussion, or checked the status of an electronic publication

Activity — Whether you posted a message, placed an ad, or modified a storefront, for example

Document name — The specific subject line or file name of a message you posted or a document you uploaded to a library

Service — The portion of cyberspace where the activity was performed, such as the Web, America Online, or a particular bulletin board system, perhaps

Path name — The specific name of a forum and forum library, the name of a discussion group, the URL of a Web page, or the phone number and keyword of the location on a bulletin board where the activity took place

Notes — Any notes you might make about how often the item should be checked or updated, when a change should be made in the future, and so on.

By tracking this information in a database program, you can easily sort on the Latest Date field to find out when you last did what. For example, each week you can easily select activity records for the previous week or month and then check the Activity fields in them to see whether these areas need your attention again.

You'll also know how to find a document or message that needs to be updated at any given time. For instance, if you know that a biographical file you uploaded to several places needs to be updated, you can easily search the Document Name field of your activity log to find out where copies of that file are located.

An activity log gives you a complete picture of your attack as it proceeds, and it helps you keep all your information up-to-date. Cyberspace is crowded with the rotting hulks of old, outdated files and messages. Some forum libraries contain files that are years old. Outdated messages send the wrong messages to your customers, so maintain a log and check it frequently.

9 MAILBOXES, FOLDERS, GROUPS, AND DIRECTORIES

Conducting an online marketing attack is like going fishing. You cast your net for new customers and then reap the benefits of your labors. But because there's so much going on in cyberspace, it can be hard to hang on to the leads or information you get through your efforts. Without some good organizational tools, your fishing net can be full of holes.

Your computer was made for organizing information. Use its capabilities to capture and store the information you get so you can make the most if it. There are two main types of information you'll want to capture and organize: e-mail addresses and information resources.

E-mail addresses. Most of the people who send you e-mail are prospects for future business. You should have some way of storing the addresses from incoming e-mail, because these addresses are the basis of your online mailing list.

The simplest thing to do is to store all those incoming e-mail messages in one place on your disk — perhaps in a separate folder, directory, or e-mail box (if your mail program allows you to create multiple mailboxes). But it is even better to *categorize* incoming e-mail addresses to give yourself a head start on using those resources the next time you make contact.

For example, one mailbox or directory might be only for messages asking about a particular product or service of yours. If the Club T-Shirt Company is participating in several different discussion groups in the hope of selling custom shirts to members of each group, it might categorize its incoming e-mail by the name of the discussion group from which the request came. That way, when the company plans a special promotional mailing in the future, it can tailor its message to each particular club and send that message to all the club's members.

Information resources. As you participate in discussion groups each day, you'll come across references to interesting Net resources, competitive sites, and potential prospects. It's important to capture these resources as you come upon them, because you'll never remember to go back to them (or where you saw them) later on.

To store this kind of information, keep a separate text file or word-processing document open at all times and copy interesting URLs, mailing list references, or other Net resources into it as you find them. As the list grows, make a commitment to yourself to check out a few items at the top of the list each week.

Without the proper organizational tools, a lot of good information and potential profits will slip through your fingers every time you go online. But with the right tools, you can capture information as you come across it and store it in a way that gives you a head start on your next marketing salvo.

10 HOT LISTS

With all the interesting discussion groups, forums, and Web sites out there in cyberspace, it's hard to keep track of everything easily. Even a casual Net user may have a dozen or more favorite places he returns to again and again. Use your Web browser, online service software, and newsreader software to store frequently visited locations so you don't have to remember and retype them each time.

Every online service has a "hot list" or "favorite places" function that lets you put any location on the service on a special menu so you can return to it easily. Your Worldwide Web browser, FTP program, and newsreader program also have bookmark functions that let you store the addresses of frequently visited locations. The sooner you learn to make use of these weapons, the more time you'll save in navigating the Net and the more time you'll have for marketing activities.

The downside of using hot lists and menus is that they can become so cluttered that it's hard to find the item you want. Every month or so, check your hot lists and bookmark menus and remove any items you really don't use often.

Another problem with Web browsers and FTP programs is that they store bookmarks according to the name of the actual resource. Unfortunately, some resources don't have very descriptive names, and over time you may forget what a bookmark name refers to. In cases like this, you may want to make a note in your Web browser's bookmark window to explain what the resource really is. If your Web browser or FTP program doesn't allow you to store a description along with a bookmark, create a "cheat sheet" with your word processor that lists important resource names and describes each one.

11 CANNED MESSAGES

Canned messages or electronic brochures are e-mail letters that you prepare in advance and have ready to send out when online prospects ask you who you are and what you do. Every guerrilla has a printed brochure ready to mail out to anyone who requests it. As an online guerrilla, you should prepare one or more canned messages that serve as electronic brochures to describe you, your company, and your products and services.

Once you go online and begin participating in discussion groups (see *Discussion group memberships*, p. 30), your contributions will generate leads. Other members of the group who like what you have to say will send you e-mail asking you for more information about your company. With an arsenal of canned messages, you can respond to these requests for information very quickly instead of having to prepare a new response each time. So before you even begin your marketing attack, prepare at least one e-mail message that describes your business and have it ready to mail out.

Canned messages will save you a lot of time. With specific messages ready to go, you can respond quickly to requests for information. Your speedy response will identify you as a well-organized professional, and you'll be that much further down the path to a rewarding business relationship. Canned messages can also help preserve your reputation. It's much better to send out a carefully crafted electronic brochure than it is to dash off a reply in the heat of the moment. Hastily written messages often contain typos or other errors, and they seldom have the clarity and focus of a well-considered brochure. Since a reply message of this type is often your first and best chance to begin a business relationship, it should also be your best effort.

Whenever you send out a canned message, however, take the time to personalize it. Guerrillas always try to make personal contacts with their customers, and that means adding a personalized greeting and perhaps an introductory sentence or two to each canned message you send out. With a personalized greeting, your customers will know that you care about them individually.

3

Presence

YOUR ONLINE MARKETING attack begins in earnest when you establish a *presence*. An online presence is both physical and psychological. The physical part is a point of contact, such as an e-mail address or a storefront, where people can reach you or get information about your company. But with millions of inhabitants and thousands of businesses competing for attention, a physical presence isn't enough for success in cyberspace. You also need to create and maintain a presence in your customers' minds. To do this, you must establish a unique electronic personality or identity that your customers associate with you and your company, and you must gain exposure for that identity as often as possible.

In this chapter, we'll examine ten weapons you can use to establish and maintain both aspects of your online presence.

12 E-MAIL ADDRESS

Anyone who is serious about doing business online has an e-mail address. E-mail is the main method of communication among cybercitizens, and it is the only communications medium you can use to reach anyone in the online world.

Your e-mail address is established automatically when you get an online account. The address consists of your user name on the particular network you use to connect with cyberspace, followed by an "at" sign (@) and the *domain name*, which identifies the network. For example, Charles Rubin's e-mail address on America Online is *crubin@aol.com*. His user name on America Online is *crubin*, and America Online's domain name is *aol.com*. (For more on domain names, see *Domain name* on p. 25.)

When you sign up for an online account, you usually get to choose your own user name, although some networks assign you a

numeric name instead. If you have a choice, pick a name that identifies you or your business. If you're just starting out and you plan to
do all your business out of one e-mail address for the foreseeable
future, choose a user name that identifies the business. Here are
some examples:

> *gladrags@aol.com*
> *automan@prodigy.com*
> *insure_me@ix.netcom.com.*

If you're starting out with one e-mail address but hope eventually
to have your own network domain name with e-mail addresses for
several key employees, then you might pick your own name as a user
name. For example, if you choose the domain name *gladrags.com,*
you'll identify each employee, department, or a mailbot with its own
user name, like this:

> *roger@gladrags.com*
> *janice@gladrags.com*
> *sales@gladrags.com*
> *info@gladrags.com*

You can't always predict how large and successful your business
will be, so you could very well choose a company name as your
initial e-mail address and then use it as your domain name, changing
gladrags@aol.com to a series of addresses at *gladrags.com,* for example. User names must be unique on each network, but you can have
the same user name on several different networks (*roger@aol.com,*
roger@ix.netcom.com, etc.). And unless someone else has already
registered a user name like *gladrags,* you can take it and register it as
a domain name later.

Whatever route you take, try to choose a name that's easy to spell
and easy to remember. One simple typo in the address will make any
mail coming to you undeliverable, so deciding on a long or difficult
user name places an extra barrier between you and potential profits.
In particular, stay away from names with numbers, underline characters, or special keyboard symbols in them — most people find
these harder to type than normal letters.

13 SIGNATURE

Wherever you get an online account, you'll be able to affix a *signature* to the end of each message you send via e-mail or post to an Internet newsgroup. Attaching a signature to your mail or discussion group postings is a standard practice in cyberspace. If your messages and postings contain useful information, people who read them will see your name and company name at the bottom and know how to reach you to ask for further information.

Your signature is an electronic business card, and as such is a very important weapon in your marketing arsenal. It should contain your name, your business name, and your contact information, and it may also contain a marketing slogan. Here are some examples:

```
Charles Rubin, coauthor, "Guerrilla Marketing Online"
crubin@sedona.net - http://www.sedona.net/crubin
1125 W. Hwy 89A, Suite 1140, Sedona, AZ 86336
800-357-1057 (dial code 33) - fax 520-204-1190
```

```
<=======================================>
Karen Conrad • Internet Publishing Professionals
"Designing Effective Storefronts Since the Web Was Born"
145 South K Street, Suite 1125, Washington, DC 10020
kconrad@ipubpro.com - http://www.ipubpro.com/home.html
      800-555-1234 • fax 202-555-1123
<=======================================>
```

```
///////////////////////////////////////////////////////////////
\\\ Bob Martinez - Old Mexico Folk Art Company    \\\
\\\\\\ Authentic Latin Handcrafts Since 1975    \\\\\\
\\ BobMart@insd.net - 800-555-1456/fax 505-555-9980    \\
\\\\ For our free catalog, e-mail FOLKART@insd.net    \\\\
///////////////////////////////////////////////////////////////
```

Each of these signatures identifies the person and the company or business and offers several different means of contact. Your signature should list all the ways you want to be available to your customers, including a phone number, fax number, mailing address, e-mail address, mailbot address, and Worldwide Web address, if you have them.

Using a signature is the one way you can promote your business anytime, anywhere, without any risk of offending people who read your messages. As you can see from these examples, you can use keyboard characters to outline your contact information, and you can also use characters to create logos or graphics inside your card. When you use such characters, you have to be careful, though (see *Logo* on p. 28).

You should have at least one business card for your e-mail and discussion group messages. You can create several different signatures with different slogans highlighting various products or services you offer. You can also come up with special signatures to use for a specific event, such as a promotion or contest.

Normally, you can create and store a signature right inside the e-mail or newsreader program you use, and it will be attached automatically to your messages. The better e-mail programs allow you to store two or more signatures and then choose which one to affix to each message. In some cases, though, you'll have to cut and paste the signature information from previous messages, a scrapbook file, or a dummy e-mail message that you have at hand whenever you compose messages.

As long as your signature contains appropriate company, name, and contact information, you can use it at any time without violating netiquette. But as with most marketing weapons, it's possible to overstep the bounds of what's acceptable in a signature. Follow two basic rules to make the most of a signature without overdoing it:

Don't use more than six screen lines. Signatures longer than this are often considered an imposition on your reader's time and screen space, and will do more harm than good. You should be able to include all pertinent information within four to six screen lines.

Stick to business. Don't include long quotations from your favorite poet or rock star, detailed declarations of your personal philosophy, or multiline ads about your business. Most people consider such information a waste of time, and they resent you for posting it.

Working within these guidelines, you should be able to design a memorable business card that helps establish your online presence and lets people know how to contact you.

14 DOMAIN NAME

In a cartoon in *The New Yorker* a few months ago, two dogs were sitting in front of a PC, and one of them said to the other, "On the Internet, nobody knows I'm a dog." You'll work hard to overcome the built-in anonymity of cyberspace as you establish and promote your online presence. But when it comes to leveling the playing field against larger competitors, you can use anonymity to your advantage. Having your own network domain name creates the impression that your company is large enough to have its own network. In reality, your domain name might be an electronic phantom that exists only in a directory on some Internet service provider's hard disk, but your customers will never know that.

Domain name registrations have soared recently, jumping over the 100,000 mark as companies large and small rush to claim their own unique identity in cyberspace. Large companies on the Net all have their own domain names, because each of them has a corporate network that needs its own identity. That's why you see names like *ge.com, microsoft.com,* and *apple.com.* But lately, large consumer-products companies have gone a little crazy with domain name registrations, registering product names like Velveeta, Sanka, Luvs, and Metamucil, presumably with an eye to creating separate domain addresses for each product.

Every domain name must be unique, so the number of available choices is shrinking every day. To get your own domain name, you must register it with the InterNIC (Internet Information Center). Most service providers will help you register your name for $25 to $50. You fill out a form on which you list several choices in order of preference, much as you do when ordering a personalized license plate for your car. Because of the stampede to register names, the process now takes several weeks. But once you've registered your domain name, it's yours forever, and nobody else can use it.

Once you have a domain name, you can get *domain name service* from your service provider. This means that your personal directory on the provider's server is accessed via your domain name rather than through the provider's domain name. Your real address might be *ix.netcom.com/gladrags*, but with domain name service, your address is *gladrags.com*, and any requests for Worldwide Web pages or e-mail deliveries automatically go to your directory. It looks to other cybercitizens as if you have your own network and equipment when in fact you don't.

So for a small registration fee and a small setup fee, you can look as big as General Motors on the Net, even if you're working out of your spare bedroom. A domain name gives you a lot of extra credibility for very little money.

15   WRITING ABILITY

Aside from an online connection, the ability to write well is the single most important weapon you can wield in cyberspace. Many of you reading this will stop right here, thinking, "Oh, I already know that." But if our experience is any guide, fewer than half of you can write well enough to make the most of a first impression in cyberspace.

The written word is the main method of communication in the online world. While your storefront may contain graphics, or you may offer your prospects software, video clips, or sound files to enhance your marketing presentation, good old text carries most of your marketing message. In an air war, the best pilots have the most success; in the online marketplace, the best writers have the upper hand.

And just as writing skill is an asset in cyberspace, lack of that skill is a liability. Your writing ability can make or break the effectiveness of your whole attack. Your e-mail messages, discussion group postings, storefront, or electronic publications will do you more harm than good if they don't clearly and efficiently say what you want to say.

Think about your writing as an extension of your personality, because it's your best and often only chance to create an impression on customers. Your prospects' opinion of you in cyberspace is affected by your command of the written word. You might have the greatest products or services in the world, but you'll never get a chance to sell anything if people are put off by sloppy writing or they simply don't understand what you're saying.

Most of us think we write better than we really do, so we're not very anxious to spend time and energy improving skills we already consider adequate. But big companies pay professional writers to create all of their public documents, electronic or not. You must strive for the same level of professionalism in all your writing.

Every professionally written document is correct, clear, economical, and personal.

Correct. Eliminate spelling, grammar, punctuation, and formatting errors from all your online messages. If customers think you're nonchalant about these matters, they may assume you're nonchalant about customer service too. If you're not sure of the rules, get a guide to business writing and check your work, or have it proofread by someone who really knows before you send it out.

Clear. Say exactly what you mean to say, and don't beat around the bush. Vague or ambiguous messages confuse the customer and put up a barrier to the sale. At best, vague messages will force you to waste your time and the customer's time with follow-up messages to clarify what should have been clear from the start. Read over your messages before you send, post, or publish them, and be sure they make your point.

Economical. It's much harder to write economically than not, but you should always try to make your point in as little space as possible. Everyone in cyberspace is pressed for time, because there's always more to do there than you can possibly do. If your messages are longer than necessary, they waste time, and they may trigger a subtle resentment in readers.

Personal. Infuse your message with as much of your business identity as possible, and speak directly to the individual reader. Professional writers know how to give their writing a voice — a distinct sound and point of view that make it unique. Most of the time, this means using the same words and figures of speech you use in day-to-day conversation and envisioning a specific person as your correspondent whenever you write something. The pros also know that using words like *you, we, us,* and *our* makes a message much more personal. Everyone who reads your message should hear your own voice and feel as if the message is directed specifically to him.

In a nutshell, develop a new attitude about your writing. Rather than dashing off messages without a second thought, give your writing the same care and consideration you would use in designing a print ad or reviewing the copy for a printed brochure. You'll have to invest some extra time in polishing your skills in the beginning, but you'll end up with a more professional online presence, better online credibility, and more sales.

16   LOGO

A logo helps your business stand out among thousands of others in the sea of words that is cyberspace. Most people are visually oriented and respond well to a logo in any situation, but a logo packs extra punch online because so much of what we see there is words.

You may already have a logo for your business. If so, you can adapt it for use online. If you don't have a logo, come up with one. It's a visual aid you can use in most of your online communications to identify your company instantly.

Use a logo in your storefront, in electronic publications, and in the signatures you attach to e-mail and discussion group messages. A good logo should be:

Timeless. The only way to establish a logo as the identifier of your company is to use it consistently for a long time. Choose a design that you can live with and that will reflect your company's identity for years.

Simple. Your logo should be instantly recognizable and easy to understand.

Unique. Your logo shouldn't be a knockoff of someone else's logo. You don't want people thinking it represents another company, and you don't want another company's lawyers on your back for design or trademark infringement.

Compatible. The logo should be compatible with your company's name and identity.

Recognizable. Your logo will be reproduced in many sizes, colors, and media. It should be instantly recognizable whether it's half an inch square or a foot square, and whether it's in an e-mail signature, on a Web page, or in a television ad.

Whether you have an existing logo or you're just coming up with one now, you'll have to adapt the design to the technical demands of cyberspace. You should have at least three versions.

A high-resolution version. This is the original version of the logo. It may contain several colors, and it is suitable for use in print ads, as a high-resolution graphic on a Worldwide Web page, or as part of a graphic file or video clip file that you make available for your prospects or customers to download from a storefront. This version of your logo is usually a .GIF or .JPEG format file that can be easily viewed with a Worldwide Web browser, and it can also be opened and resized with a standard graphics program.

To create an electronic version of a printed logo, you will need to scan it with a computer scanner and save the image as a .GIF or .JPEG format file. To create a logo from scratch, use a computer-based drawing or painting program.

A smaller or lower-resolution version. This is usually a separate version of the high-resolution logo. You can have your designer make it with fewer colors or with a looser halftone screen, or you might be able to use a scanner to create it. You can also create a smaller version of your high-resolution logo.

The smaller the image or the lower its resolution, the smaller the disk file that contains it. Smaller files can be displayed more quickly online than large files, because it takes less time to transfer them. For example, a high-resolution logo might occupy 50K or more of disk space, and it may take more than ten seconds to display with a Worldwide Web browser if the user has a typical modem connection. In contrast, a low-resolution or half-size version of the same logo might occupy only 10K or 15K of space and load three or four times as quickly.

An ASCII version. This version of your logo is made up of text characters arranged in a pattern that matches the design of your high-resolution version. E-mail and discussion group messages can't contain graphic files, so you need an ASCII version of your logo that can be transmitted along with your text. Here's an example:

```
——(oo)——Broadway Costume House - "Spooks A Specialty"
——/\\——1125 N. Broadway, Oakland, CA 94610
——//—\\——510-555-1111 - fax: 510-555-1112
——//——\\—info@disguise.com - http://www.disguise.com
```

This company has used the underline (_), backslash (\), slash (/), and lowercase "o" characters to create an ASCII version of its logo. You can use other keyboard symbols to create pictures, too.

When designing an ASCII graphic, keep in mind that the font and font size you use on your computer may not be the same as those used in your recipients' e-mail programs. Your logo must be designed so that changes in font or font size won't affect the alignment of the characters on the screen. Here are four ways to help ensure that your logo will look the same to everyone who views it.

First, use only one space character between other characters in the graphic. Don't use multiple spaces to align characters on your screen, because the spaces will be different sizes on other computers, and the alignment will be thrown off accordingly.

Second, don't use special symbols that aren't part of the standard ASCII character set, such as bullets, foreign language symbols, and so on. Your computer may have symbols that are specific to a particular font, but you're safe using any symbol that's displayed on your keyboard.

Third, don't rely on tabs, indents, centering, or other alignment shortcuts to arrange the characters in your logo. These formatting elements are stripped away when your logo is sent via e-mail or posted to a discussion group. If you create the logo inside your e-mail or newsreader program, formatting shortcuts aren't available anyway.

Finally, when you've finished designing your ASCII logo, try viewing it with different fonts and font sizes to make sure it looks the same in every case.

With appropriate versions of your logo at the ready, get in the habit of using them consistently. An effective logo used regularly will enhance your company's identity in any Internet communication.

17   DISCUSSION GROUP MEMBERSHIPS

Your e-mail box and your e-mail signature won't ever be seen by anyone if you sit passively by and wait for someone to write to you. You must make others aware of your online presence by getting your name and signature in front of as many potential customers as possible.

The best way to get online visibility is to join one or more discussion groups. Discussion groups are forums on online services or bulletin board systems; mailing lists (where the discussion is an exchange of e-mail messages among subscribers to a list); or newsgroups on the Internet. There are thousands and thousands of discussion groups, each of which is oriented to a specific topic.

Discussion group participation is the most effective way to locate and develop a relationship with your online customers. Here are the six steps to discussion group marketing, guerrilla style.

1. Selection finds your customers. The first step is to find a discussion group that will suit your marketing purposes. Ideally, the group's members should be regularly discussing issues or asking for advice about subjects that you specialize in for your business.

To find appropriate discussions in which to participate, first search the list of available newsgroups with your newsreader program's Find or Search command, or browse in the list in your Full Group List window. Look for groups whose names have something to do with your marketing purposes and then read a few of the messages in the group to find out if the topics of discussion are related to your business.

Then search a list of mailing list discussions. You'll find a list of these on your online service, and there are several of them on the Worldwide Web. On the Web, use a Web searching tool to search for *Mailing Lists*, and you'll be pointed in the right direction.

The next thing is to browse in the discussion group list on your online service and look for groups related to your area of business.

Finally, check a list of bulletin board systems and look for ones that are related to your business area. Online services usually have lists of bulletin board systems, and a discussion group on the Net called *alt.bbs.lists* has them, too.

2. The FAQ tells you the ground rules. When you locate a group that looks promising for your marketing purposes, see if there's an FAQ (Frequently Asked Questions) message that explains more about it. Internet newsgroups and forums on online services usually have information files that tell you who the group's administrator is, what kinds of messages are allowed and prohibited, and what subjects of discussion are encouraged.

3. Lurking shows you how to participate. You can find out about nearly any discussion group by *lurking*, or reading the messages posted to it for a week or two. You'll find out who the group's regular members are, what they're talking about, and what kinds of messages are encouraged or discouraged. This initial research is essential, because it gives you a good sense of how to join in the discussion when you decide to step out into the spotlight. Make sure you know the ropes of a discussion before joining it, because it's hard to repair a bad first impression.

4. Participating gives you visibility. Once you're familiar with the group's discussion topics and its general rules of participation, become an active member by joining in. Comment on a message someone else has posted, answer questions other people pose, propose new topics of discussion on your own, or post a message alerting the group's members to a new resource you've found. The quality of your messages will determine your reputation as a member of the group. If you're a true guerrilla, you'll make sure that the messages are all very interesting and useful to the other members of the group, and you'll also make sure that every message ends with a signature identifying you and your company and saying how to reach you.

Your goal is to make such a positive impression on the other members of the group that the next time they have a need for your product or service, yours is the first company that comes to mind. You don't do this by posting advertisements for your business (which are usually prohibited in discussions). Instead, you do it by giving away useful information and becoming a respected member of the group. If you can earn members' respect, they will seek you out for future business via the information in your signature.

5. Providing useful information gives you credibility. It's easy to gain visibility in a discussion by posting messages to it, but if you want to gain the credibility you'll need to attract business, be careful to provide solid, useful information every time you post a message.

Here are some dos and don'ts that will help you offer the right kinds of information in a discussion.

Do describe your message with a clear subject line. Nobody likes to have to open message after message just to find out what they're about. Your subject line should clearly explain what the subject of your message is.

Don't post advertisements. Most discussions forbid these anyway, and even if you slip one through, you'll probably generate a lot of flames or hate mail. (However, some discussion groups are actually message boards for classified ads. See p. 84 in Chapter 6.)

Do express your point of view about existing message topics, as long as you have something new to add to the discussion. If someone expresses an opinion and you disagree, post a response to it. If someone asks for comments about a new topic, make a comment if you can contribute something useful. If someone asks a question that you can answer, post a reply to the question.

Don't agree for the sake of agreement. It's important to participate frequently in a discussion if you want to maintain visibility, but don't reply to messages or post new ones that simply repeat and agree with what someone else has said. "Me too" messages are a waste of time for everybody who reads them.

Don't argue for the sake of argument. Once all sides of an issue have been discussed, don't beat it into the ground. Every discussion has one or more members who insist on having the last word on a topic, but they too develop reputations as time-wasters.

Do think about the length, format, and content of your messages. The most effective discussion group messages are concise and to the point. Before you post a message, read it over and think about whether you can get your point across more clearly and efficiently.

Don't belabor the obvious or diverge onto unrelated topics. Nobody likes to read messages where the author repeats the same point or gets sidetracked onto a totally different subject.

Do share information resources with other group members. It's helpful to point group members to articles, directories, Net searching tools, and other resources you've discovered.

Don't post long articles. If you find a good article and you want to share it with the group, it's better to post a short excerpt and then tell people where they can see the rest than it is to post the entire article.

Do start new topics of discussion. If you can think of a topic that showcases your area of expertise more clearly and it's not being discussed, bring it up as a new point of discussion. If you have a question that the group might help with, ask it.

Don't try to disguise an advertisement as a new discussion topic.

Remember that discussion topics are meant to draw group members into an exchange of ideas, not to get them to visit your Web page. For example, asking about how to handle negotiations with a Web site developer would provoke a discussion. In contrast, announcing your Web site or posting your product literature and asking for critiques of them are obvious, self-serving attempts to boost your visitation or readership.

Do invite private e-mail exchanges. If you have more to say about a topic that relates specifically to the author of a particular message, send that person a direct e-mail message and suggest a private exchange.

6. Consistency builds relationships. Participating in a discussion is like going on the radio or TV; the minute you're off the air, people begin forgetting you. The only way to maintain your presence in a discussion is to participate regularly and consistently. Make sure you take part in a discussion at least once a week, if possible, and take care that all your messages reinforce your business identity.

Participating in discussion groups seems like a time-consuming and inefficient way to generate business on the Net, but it only seems that way. People who think nothing of spending most of their day on the phone or in the store helping customers and answering questions somehow balk at spending a few minutes doing the same thing online. But remember, every positive, helpful message you post to a discussion group is read by dozens or hundreds of people. Being a discussion group member is actually a much more effective way of polishing your reputation than making the one-to-one contacts you normally make off-line.

18   STOREFRONT

A storefront is any fixed location on the Net where you can display information about your company, offer samples of your products or services, and generally present information to anyone who visits. Technically, a storefront is a collection of files at a specific location on a server connected to the online world somehow. That location might be space you rent on an Internet service provider's system, a store you rent on an online service like America Online or CompuServe, a place on a bulletin board system connected to the Net, a server at a university or government agency, or a server on your own corporate network.

A storefront is a potent weapon for creating an online presence, because it runs twenty-four hours a day, seven days a week without your intervention. It's a great way to tell the online market about your business with a minimum of hassle on your part. Rather than asking you to e-mail them more information about your business, cybernauts can simply visit your storefront and learn about it there. And depending on the kind of storefront you choose, the information you provide can be text, pictures, sounds, video clips, or software.

Despite all the potential of storefronts, most online businesses aren't making the most of them. There are three basic goals to keep in mind while you choose and develop an effective storefront.

Serve a specific need.

Your storefront should have a specific purpose that supports your overall business mission. Here are some specific needs you might serve:

Lower marketing costs. You might set up a storefront to cut down information distribution costs, since posting information on a storefront is much less expensive than printing it and mailing it, or than paying someone to give it out over the telephone.

Faster information distribution. You can update information on a storefront from one minute to the next, much more quickly than if you had to reprint brochures or catalogs. Several sports-oriented sites on the Worldwide Web, for example, now offer play-by-play coverage in real time.

Better customer service. With a storefront, you give customers access to information and services twenty-four hours a day, seven days a week. You can enable them to place orders, check on the status of orders, browse in an online catalog, or leave messages for members of your staff whenever they choose. Giving customers more control over when and where they make a purchase is one of the best ways to increase your business.

More sales. With a storefront that's available to people all over the world, you can present your products or services to whole new markets that you couldn't afford to reach in other ways. Flower shops, specialty food vendors, and other businesses in the United States have expanded sales into Europe, Asia, and Latin America by making their products available on the Net.

Have one (or more) of these needs firmly in mind when you choose a location and a design for your storefront, and make sure you're doing all you can to address that need.

Offer a unique advantage.

Most people spend most of their time off-line, and shopping in particular represents a very small part of the activity in cyberspace. In order to be successful, your storefront must offer a unique advantage that brings customers to it. Many storefronts on the Net these days are simply recreations of a printed brochure, catalog, or magazine ad. Your storefront must do more, or people will have no reason to visit it. (And even if you can get them to visit it once, they'll have no reason to return.)

Ideally, your storefront should be so great that your customers would get an online account just to be able to visit it. Few stores meet that lofty goal, but if you're aiming for it, at least you'll be headed in the right direction. Here are some of the advantages you might try to offer:

Expertise and information. The low cost of publishing information in a storefront allows you to offer much more of it than you can in print. You can offer detailed instructions for using products, analyses of trends affecting your customers, directories of information resources your customers regularly need, lists of frequently asked questions, and other types of information. By having all the information your customers need in one convenient place, your store becomes a resource rather than just a place that sells things.

Communication. By hosting a message board or offering e-mail links to key employees at your company, you can make it much easier for your customers to comment on your products, ask questions, and get answers. A message board creates a virtual community where people who use your products or services can meet to discuss their experience. The continuous nature of the discussion helps keep visitors coming back to your store once they've found it. Check out http://www.well.com or http://www.books.com for examples of Web sites that offer discussions.

Interactive training. With text and graphics, you can offer weekly lessons about your area of expertise. For example, the Ragu Spaghetti Sauce site on the Worldwide Web (http://www.eat.com) offers one weekly lesson in speaking Italian and another in Italian culture.

Order tracking. Companies like Book Stacks Unlimited (http://www.books.com) and Federal Express (http://www.fedex.com) enable customers to track the status of an order or shipment right from their Worldwide Web storefronts. You could also allow customers or field sales employees to check your inventory and find out whether or not an item is in stock. Thanks to the ease of updating information on a storefront, these services are less expensive to offer on the Net — you don't have to pay an employee to look this information up for each customer or salesperson who needs it — and they're available for your customers or employees to use at any time of the day or night.

Instant quotations or reports. Set up a form on which customers can specify items to order and then get a quote on the price, or offer a page that shows the daily price of commodities like lumber or soybeans. You might also enable customers to calculate the cost of an auto lease, mortgage, or consumer loan.

The best way to come up with a unique advantage for your storefront is to think about the services or characteristics of your business that make it successful off-line and then leverage the power of the Net to improve them online. If your customers can get the same information just as quickly off-line, then they have no reason to visit you in cyberspace. But if you can offer a distinct advantage that's useful to both your company and your customers, the storefront will be a success.

Be visible and accessible to your target audience.

The most useful storefront in the world will fail if your customers don't know about it or can't access it. So a final point to consider when choosing a location for your storefront is to be sure that your customers can get to it. If, for example, you're hoping to expand your market nationally or overseas, you won't want to choose a storefront on a local bulletin board system that people will have to make a long-distance call to connect with. Similarly, you wouldn't want to choose a storefront on America Online or another commercial service that isn't available in most countries.

However, if your storefront is meant to increase your business within a local geographical area, then putting it on the Worldwide Web might attract inquiries from customers around the world whom you can't possibly serve. In this case, a bulletin board system with a local phone number would be better.

If few of your customers are online now, plan to bring them online by offering a terrific service through your storefront. Choose a storefront that people can access as easily as possible and then give your customers a free software disk that gets them online with a few mouse clicks. By working with a local Internet service provider, for example, you could distribute an Internet access kit with a Worldwide Web browser preconfigured to go directly to your company's home page when users start it up each time. If you set up a bulletin board system, you could distribute a graphical access program for it so customers can connect simply by choosing a command.

Once you've chosen the kind of storefront that is most accessible for your customers or employees, plan to promote it. We discuss promotional weapons in Chapters 6 and 7, but a storefront can't do its job if nobody visits it. And nobody will visit your store unless they know where it is and are motivated to go there.

As part of your storefront plan, develop a promotional plan that gives your store visibility. You'll want members of relevant discussion groups, Web surfers visiting related Web sites, readers of relevant magazines, and other audiences to hear about your storefront and become curious enough to visit. If your customers aren't online now, you'll need to promote your site and your free access software in your physical store or through direct mail.

19 STOREFRONT DESIGN

Simply having a storefront in cyberspace is no guarantee of success. Lots of storefronts out there actually turn customers away rather than attracting them because they don't offer anything useful or the information is too difficult to get. A good storefront design enhances your business identity, provides useful information in a convenient way, and encourages return visits. Here are some keys to a successful design.

Make it clear.

Many storefronts in cyberspace are confusing because their opening page, or "home page," doesn't tell visitors what the store is about. Typically, confusing stores have just a company name or logo or a large graphic or *image map* that appears when visitors navigate to it. Unless the company's name is a household word, the name doesn't tell visitors anything. And even if it is a household word, it alone won't tell visitors what they can expect to see or do by visiting the store.

Every storefront's main page should be like the sign or window in a retail store. It should identify the business and briefly say what visitors can see or do if they move further into the store. The Internet is not a treasure hunt, and there are so many storefronts out there to choose from that visitors won't take the time to dig into a site unless they have reason to believe that their efforts will be rewarded.

If you're designing a Worldwide Web storefront, don't confuse customers by using graphics on your home page without any text to go along with them. Most people who spend any time at all on the Web have their browser program set so that images aren't automatically loaded. It's much faster to surf the Web without waiting for graphics to load at every turn.

When your home page is all graphics, visitors only see a group of generic icons or boxes when they visit with image-loading off in their Web browser programs. As a result, they probably won't know what the site is, how to navigate in it, or why they should want to. To learn any of these things, they will have to load the site's images and wait half a minute or more in the process.

It's much better to include some text on your home page that covers the basics. If the graphics on your site are identified with text captions and they look interesting, your visitors can always choose to load them later.

The most egregious examples of "over-graphication" on Web sites occur because the site's look has been entirely determined by a graphic designer. Graphic designers like lots of pictures, but lots of pictures are a problem on the Web. Don't let your graphic designer determine the function of your Web site! Forcing your customers to wait half a minute or more to load a bunch of graphics just to find out what the store is and how to navigate in it is like greeting first-time visitors to your office with a pitchfork.

Advances in graphics rendering and Net access speeds will make it easier to use larger and more interesting graphics on the Net in the future. But it's too early to assume that everyone on the Net can see or wants to see them now. If you've developed a store where the graphics are really spectacular and important, offer a separate, text-only view of the store for those who can't see graphics or don't want to look at them. The customers' needs come first, so give them a choice.

Make it easy.

Your storefront's organization should be logical and self-evident. The names of departments listed on your home page should be descriptive, and if possible they should be evocative enough so that people will want to check them out. *What's New* sounds better than *About This Site*, for example. *Shop In Our Store* sounds better than *Display Catalog*. And when you list products in a catalog and want to include a link to your order form, use a name like *I Want It!* instead of *Go To Online Order Form*. Try to arouse curiosity and excitement with the language in your online store, but be careful not to cause confusion.

Make it fast.

Time is the most precious commodity for a Net surfer. Sitting in front of a computer screen and waiting for data or a graphic to appear is agonizing, so your storefront should deliver information as quickly as possible.

If you use lots of graphics, make sure you include some text on every page. That way, the text will load quickly and people will have something to look at while waiting for graphics to load on the same page (if they've chosen to view the graphics).

Avoid graphics larger than 30K or so in size unless they're absolutely essential to your presentation. If large graphics are necessary, try displaying smaller, "thumbnail" versions of them and then giving your visitors the option of viewing the larger versions. Use a small text caption below each big graphic that indicates how large it is, so customers can make an informed choice about whether or not to wait for it to load.

Break up information onto multiple pages rather than cramming it all onto one long page. It's easier and more natural for people to click a link or a direction button to move from page to page than it is to scroll endlessly down one long document on the screen. Smaller pages also load more quickly than large ones, so it saves your visitors time to break your information up.

Make it interesting.

Text is the main method of expression in a storefront, but that doesn't automatically mean your store will be boring. There are lots of ways to make visiting your store a unique experience.

- Use evocative, people-oriented words to describe your company, your store, and its departments.
- Use small graphics to break up pages visually and create a mood.
- Come up with an overall voice and identity for the store that matches your company identity. For a great example of this, see the Ragu Spaghetti Sauce site at http://www.eat.com.

Design for return visits.

Repetition is a key to maintaining your online identity. Encouraging return visits to your store builds in repeated exposure to your company name and message. The best way to encourage return visits is to have at least one element of your storefront that changes frequently, and to make sure customers find out about it right away, the first time they visit. Some changing store departments might be:

- A weekly industry news update
- A weekly tip or lesson about your product or service
- A discussion group where visitors can post messages
- A "What's New" area that lists the recent changes to your store.

Design for buying comfort.

Mail-order is a fifty-billion-dollar-a-year business, and right now Internet sales are less than one percent of that amount. Buying and selling via computer is a new and scary experience for most people. Online guerrillas address the fear problem head-on by going out of their way to enhance customer comfort. Here are some of the tactics you can use to increase comfort in your storefront design.

Debunk the security myth. Credit card information transferred via e-mail or otherwise over the Net is really just as secure as information given to a salesperson on the phone or in a store or restaurant. Online shoppers need to know this, so you should point it out as part of your ordering information.

Offer a no-hassle guarantee. Mail-order never took off until customers had a money-back guarantee, and Net sales won't take off until guarantees become common there, too. (See *Guarantee* on p. 64 in Chapter 5.)

Explain the ordering process. Many electronic shoppers are novices at online ordering, so your ordering department should explain the whole process. Tell customers what they should do to fill out a form and transmit an order, how and when the order is transmitted, when they should expect a confirmation of the order, and how quickly the order will be shipped. (See *Order Form* on p. 60 in Chapter 5.)

Make your business tangible. Your storefront is really just a ghost in cyberspace. Do everything you can to impress customers with your professionalism and stability. If your company has been in business for a few years, list an establishment date so they will know you didn't go into business yesterday. If you have a physical address for your business, include that in your signature or on your home page as well. Offer a short business history and brief biographies of your main employees. Even if customers don't read your company history, they'll know it's there.

Act like you're ready to do business. A good storefront is always under construction, because you're always thinking about how you can improve the design and add services or information to it. But that doesn't mean your customers should need hardhats, or that they should be inconvenienced by your changes. If you're planning a new department for your store, for example, don't list it on your main menu until the department is ready to visit. It doesn't make any sense to offer a new link on your home page if the only result of clicking it is a page that says, "Under Construction." Doing this is wasting your customers' time. And if you move or rearrange pages on your storefront, make sure everything works properly after you do.

Test it.

Lots of storefronts look great in the design stage, but something is lost in the translation to an active Net presence. Files are misplaced, directory names are misspelled, graphics are lost. Before you begin promoting your storefront among your customers, make sure everything in the store works the way you expect it to. Click on each of the links or icons in the storefront to make sure it works. Examine every page to be certain it shows what you really want to display without errors or omissions. Customers have little patience with sites that don't perform as advertised.

20 PACKAGING

Every company has a package, a physical presence it communicates to the outside world. Guerrillas use packaging to reinforce their business identity, reputation, and visibility in the online marketplace. A good package should inspire confidence, enhance your identity, and distinguish you among your competitors.

Most of us think of packaging as the physical carton or box that contains products, but it's much more than that. Some aspects of your online packaging include:

- Your signature
- Your storefront
- Canned messages
- Online publications
- Discussion group messages
- Your order form
- Order confirmations
- Diskette labels.

All these items should have a consistent visual identity so that any time customers see one of them, they instantly relate it to your other online marketing efforts. For example, all of your canned e-mail messages or publications should have the same look, just as all of your printed letters go out on the same letterhead and have the same formatting. The spacing, arrangement, and content of your company name, contact information, and logo should be consistent in all the items mentioned above.

Packaging is a subtle art, but your skill should rapidly improve as you begin using this weapon to set your business apart from the crowd.

21 REPETITION

Repetition is an important factor in any advertising or marketing campaign. It fixes your identity in the customer's mind, and it promotes a feeling of stability. Studies have shown that a prospective customer must see your message twenty-seven times before he or she decides to do business with you.

Off-line advertisers repeat their messages by making them part of the environment. They post their company name and theme or logo on billboards, transit benches, taxis, sports stadiums, store displays, and signs. They also buy display ads in magazines and newspapers, and on radio and TV. They put their name on keychains, pens, coffee mugs, T-shirts, and baseball hats and then give these items away to anyone who wants one. Because of the media diversity in the off-line world, many people get repetitive messages about a company almost subliminally while commuting to work, channel surfing, visiting friends, or listening to the radio in the back yard.

On the Net, you don't have as many options for repeating your message. It's very difficult to make your messages part of the landscape in the online marketplace (but see *Sponsorships* on p. 108). Still, repetition is vital, so you must work hard to keep your company name and message in front of your target audience.

One way to repeat is to attach a signature to every e-mail message or discussion group message you send. Others are to participate frequently in one or more discussion groups, to publish electronically, to attend online conferences, to have a storefront, and to use many of the other weapons covered in this book. But no matter how or where you seek visibility, there are three cardinal rules to keep in mind.

Inappropriate visibility is worse than no visibility. You can get a lot of visibility by simply posting the same advertisement to every news-group on the Internet, but doing so will do your reputation more harm than good. Avoid mass e-mailings, mass postings to discussions, and indiscriminate placement of your messages. Every location you seek for visibility should be one where your message will reach prospective customers and be welcomed by them.

An inconsistent message confuses customers. As you go about placing messages in cyberspace, make sure every single one of them reinforces your business identity and conveys the same key market-ing messages. Otherwise, your efforts at visibility will result in more confusion than customers.

Don't stop looking for more visibility. The online landscape changes constantly. The continuing challenge for guerrillas is to keep searching for appropriate places to contribute or publish infor-mation, to add a directory listing, or to use the other visibility-related weapons discussed throughout this book.

4
Service

ADVERTISING, PROMOTION, LOCATION, and luck may bring you customers, but it takes service to keep them. Service is everything you do to make things easy on your customers when they do business with you.

Very few businesses can really claim to offer a unique product, dramatically lower prices, or a broader selection of products than their competitors. Most businesses, large and small, rely on service to turn one-time shoppers into repeat customers. In fact, a large portion of the world's economy involves businesses that compete on the basis of service: banking, insurance, accounting, law, delivery, transportation, and health care, to name a few of them. Even businesses that appear to compete mainly on price, quality, or location — supermarkets, gas stations, muffler shops, dry cleaners, and restaurants, for example — use service to maintain a steady stream of repeat customers.

Guerrillas understand the link between service and repeat business. They know that outstanding service is the most important competitive factor. This is especially true on the Net, where worldwide access and stiff competition often reduce or eliminate the advantages of such factors as price, selection, or location.

In the online marketplace, service begins the minute a customer decides to get more information about your product or service. Your business should be easy to learn about, whether you distribute information via e-mail or from a storefront. Information should be easy to find, easy to get, and easy to understand. If you distribute it through a storefront, your storefront should be easy to navigate in as well.

Once a customer has found you, the Internet can be a scary place to do business. Your customers can't see or talk to you on the Net, and they're likely to ask questions and place orders on faith. They provide a credit card number on the assumption that it will reach you safely, that it won't be misused, and that their order will be handled quickly and efficiently.

If you're a true guerrilla, you'll knock yourself out to deliver prompt, reliable, and consistent service. In doing so, you'll make the Net a friendlier place for your customers. You'll develop a reputation for rock-solid reliability that your customers will rely on, and it will be a formidable defense against your competition.

In this chapter, we'll look at nine weapons you can use to boost the quality of your service on the Net.

22 HOURS AND DAYS OF OPERATION

The Internet is available twenty-four hours a day, seven days a week. Your business should be, too. When customers ask you for information or place orders on the Net, they have no way of knowing whether you received their request until you respond. The more quickly you respond, the more confidence your customers will have in you.

Your online hours and days of operation are a matter of availability and responsiveness. You can't be on the Net twenty-four hours a day, but you can easily spend a couple of minutes a few times every day to check for new business opportunities and respond to them. Some cybernauts are online only at night, and others are online only on weekends. Each country has its own holidays, and international time zones can mean it's Monday in Asia or Australia when it's Sunday where you live.

Many Net-based businesses lose customers because they don't respond quickly enough. When MCI began promoting its Internet access service, the company was slow to distribute its information packets via snail mail. By the time MCI got around to responding, many prospective customers had signed up with someone else.

Naturally, you can't respond to something if you're not aware of it. Having an e-mail account and checking it regularly are two very different things, and many of today's netizens assume that simply having an account keeps them in touch. If you or your company has an e-mail account, you may not be checking it often enough. But with frequent checks and rapid responses, you can offer amazing service for your customers and scoop the competition.

Here's an example. Suppose your competitor checks his e-mail once a day, at 9:00 A.M., and you check yours four times a day, at 9:00 A.M., noon, 3:00 P.M., and 5:30 P.M. A prospective customer sends you and your competitor requests for information at 10:00 A.M. You respond to the request when you check your mail at noon. Your competitor doesn't find out about the request or respond to it until the next morning. If the customer needs the product or service right away, she may already have ordered from you by the time your competitor is aware he has a prospect.

Being available means checking your e-mail at least twice every day of the week, including weekends and holidays. That way, you'll be able to reply to new mail within twelve hours no matter when you receive it. Most netizens expect e-mail responses within one business day, but by responding more quickly you'll impress everyone with your professionalism and commitment.

Set your e-mail program to log on automatically twice a day or more and check for new mail. If you're going out of town, have someone else check your mail if you can't do it on the road. It only takes a few minutes of your time, and it makes a big difference to your reputation and credibility on the Net.

23 ACCESS OPTIONS

Your customers on the Net may be anywhere in the world. Customers in different countries have different kinds of access to the Net. You should be prepared to present your information in several ways to accommodate various levels of access. Some of the oldest and most successful online businesses know this. For example, Penny-Wise Office Products has storefronts on CompuServe, America Online, the Worldwide Web, and a private bulletin board system that customers can dial directly. This way, the company is accessible to subscribers of two major online services, Worldwide Web browsers on the Net, and even customers who aren't on the Net at all.

In considering how to present your business information online, think about where your customers are and how they might reach you. Here are some access options you'll want to consider.

A bulletin board system (BBS). If your market is limited to a geographical area, consider setting up a bulletin board system with a local telephone number. This way, any customer with a computer and a modem can reach you without having to sign up with an Internet service provider or an online service. For example, a local remodeling contractor might offer home repair tips or answer questions about remodeling and repairs.

If your customers have never been online, you can attract them by offering useful information on your BBS and by distributing free copies of a communications program that is preset to connect with your BBS. And if your market expands outside a local dialing area, you can still offer easy access through an 800 number or by linking your BBS to the Net and making it available via the Telnet service.

E-mail. E-mail is the only service available to everyone on the Net. Prepare e-mail versions of your brochures, order form, proposal, confirmation notice, invoice, and other standard business messages and have them ready to send out.

Individual Net storefronts. There are several types of storefronts you can choose. In deciding which way to go, think about your potential customers and how you can make sure they'll be able to find and use your storefront. You may think initially of putting up a Worldwide Web site, for example, but if you do, your information won't be available to the majority of people connected to the Net. Along with a Web site, you might also want to put your information on an FTP site, a Gopher server, or a bulletin board system, so it's available to people who can't surf the Web.

Setting up a storefront of your own requires more work on your part, but it also gives you much more control over the store's complexity, speed, and capacity to handle simultaneous customers.

Net shopping malls. Rather than setting up an independent storefront, you may choose to include your store in a service provider's mall, where several different businesses are located. Most shopping malls are Worldwide Web sites, but there are a few commercially oriented Gopher malls as well, such as the SeaGopher site in Seattle, Washington. If your customers are from a geographical region that is primarily served by the provider who maintains the mall, locating your storefront there will give you more visibility among those customers.

However, you usually pay a premium to locate inside a Net

shopping mall, and you usually must rely on (and pay for) the mall's operator to construct and maintain the store.

Storefronts on online services. Storefronts on online services such as Prodigy and CompuServe are usually much more expensive than stores in other online locations, but if that's where your primary market is, that's where the profits will be. After all, the price of a marketing program doesn't make it expensive: if a program is profitable, then it's worth whatever you spend, but the cheapest program in the world is too expensive if it doesn't increase profits.

Online services can be attractive places to do business because they may have large, well-established communities of users who are hot prospects for your business. For example, if a service has a particularly active retirees' forum and you sell products or services for seniors, it might be well worth setting up shop there. Online services also offer extra marketing help, such as announcements on their Welcome screens, billboards, and special links to forums where your products might be of particular interest.

The savviest marketers on the Net go where the customers are. Don't assume that being somewhere on the Net means you're available to everyone on the Net. Some netizens don't have access to certain services, and others don't use them even if they have them. For example, many people on America Online have access to the Worldwide Web, but they spend far more time shopping and browsing on AOL than they do venturing out onto the Web. And many people who first learn of a company on the Web will ask for more information via e-mail. If you don't limit your customers' access, you won't limit your profits.

24 CONVENIENCE

Given equal products, pricing, selection, and quality, convenience can make the difference in the race for sales. To use convenience as a weapon, develop a customer-centric attitude about your manner of doing business. Constantly evaluate your business from the customers' point of view and think about how you can make your business relationships better or easier for them.

Let's walk through the stages of customer interaction and look at some ways to improve convenience along the way.

Initial contact. Make it easy for customers to learn about your business without being intrusive. Ideally, your company name should come to mind at the exact moment when your customers need your type of product or service, and it should be easy for them to find out how to contact you.

The only way to develop that kind of identity in customers' minds is through repetition of your company name and basic marketing message. But these items should be repeated unobtrusively. Use discussion group memberships, classified ads, directory listings, electronic publishing, and conferences to get the word out about you and your business.

Rather than forcing your business on unsuspecting netizens by posting blatant ads to discussion groups, for example, participate regularly by posting useful replies or comments to relevant discussions and affix a well-designed signature to each message (see *Discussion group memberships* on p. 30). People will read your messages because of their informative content, and they'll remember your company because of the signature.

Constantly be on the lookout for opportunities to add your company name to online business directories. If you have a Web storefront, look for opportunities to trade Worldwide Web links with related sites, so your company name appears in more and more places.

Publish informative documents in places where your customers are likely to find them. Upload documents to libraries in forums related to your business. Offer to add them to Worldwide Web sites related to your business. Offer to contribute a column to online newsletters related to your business. Each of these is an opportunity to tell people what you know, who you are, and how to reach you.

Hold online conferences or chat sessions in forums related to your business or where your customers are likely to congregate. This is another way to enhance your credibility and at the same time tell people who you are and how to contact you.

In the aggregate, all these methods give you the online visibility and repetition that will create a position for your company in the customer's mind without overstepping the bounds of netiquette.

Information requests. Be prepared to learn about and respond to further requests for information as quickly and effectively as possible. Consider using a mailbot to provide instant responses to initial requests for more information about your business. Prepare a mailbot document in advance, and study the mailbot's server log once every couple of weeks to find out who is requesting your information. If you don't use a mailbot, check your e-mail two to four times a day, every day, and prepare electronic brochures in advance so you can fire off information quickly.

If your company is large enough, delegate requests for information to the appropriate person, so the most knowledgeable and helpful employee handles each customer contact.

Orders. To devise an ordering system that meets your customers' needs, think about who those customers are, where they're located, and how they might pay for your products or services.

If you're seeking international business, for example, your order form should allow for payment by internationally accepted methods such as Eurocards and JCB Cards as well as Visa and MasterCard. Make your shipping and handling rates adjustable so people overseas pay their share of the costs but not more. Work out the best possible deals on shipping so customers in remote places aren't penalized unfairly.

Another way to build convenience into the ordering process is to give customers access to information about whether or not an item is in stock, so they don't have to wait until they receive an order confirmation to learn that the item can't be shipped immediately.

Shipments. Most customers will worry about their order until they receive it. Find a way to get any item to a customer within a week at most. Many catalog firms use second-day or overnight delivery as standard practice. If you can't afford this as a standard shipping method, offer it as an option so your customers know they can speed delivery if they want to pay a little extra. Inside each package, include further marketing information, your guarantee, and instructions about your return procedure.

Repeat business. Repeat business is more profitable than new business because it costs less to develop. Your customers should benefit from their status as repeaters as well. Schedule periodic mailings about new products or services (or advice about using existing ones) and send them to existing customers. Pack as much useful information into these mailings as possible, rather than just using them as ads. Both kinds of information serve to remind customers you're still there, but with useful information the reminder comes in a package that says you care about their needs rather than yours.

You can also make repeat online sales more convenient for your customers by assigning each one an account number after his first order. Make a point of telling repeat customers that they can identify themselves on your order form simply by entering their account number, rather than by having to retype the same name, address, and credit card information. Mail-order houses use this tactic all the time to make it easier for repeaters to do business with them.

25 ACCESS SPEED

Once a customer has an interest in your business, you want to be able to satisfy that interest as quickly as possible. Mail-order and TV offers would fail if customers couldn't order instantly via an 800 number, yet a lot of online businesses make life tough on their customers by limiting the speed with which they can get information or place orders.

In the online marketplace, speed of access is affected by five factors:

- The processing speed of the server that is sending out your information;
- The speed of the connection between the server where your information is and the Net;
- The amount of data you're sending in a given transaction;
- The speed of data transfer between your server's connection and the customer's location; and
- The speed of the computer and Net connection at the customer's end.

You don't have any control over the last two variables here, but you can and should do all you can to maximize the speed of the other three. Here are some suggestions.

First, find a provider who is using a relatively fast computer system as a server, preferably a mid- to high-end UNIX workstation such as a Sun SparcStation or an SGI Indigo system. Systems like this can transfer data more quickly and handle more simultaneous users than a 486- or Pentium-based PC. In addition, find out how many other businesses are using the same server and how many simultaneous callers the system will support with reasonable speed. Even the fastest server will bog down if hundreds of people are trying to get information from it at the same time.

Naturally, you can't control the number of people accessing a server, and every service provider or online service has its peak usage periods, but by finding the providers with faster equipment, you'll be doing your part to help the situation.

When you set up a storefront, most Internet service providers should be willing to guarantee you service at a certain level — either a certain amount of data transferred per day, week, or month, or a certain number of user accesses (hits) per day, week, or month. This way, you'll have a level of service to expect and against which to measure actual performance. If the actual performance of the ISP's system falls below what you've agreed to, you may be able to renegotiate the price of service.

Next, locate your storefront, mailbot, and e-mail account with a provider or on a server connected to the Net with the fastest connection possible. You can make a rough evaluation by looking for servers connected via a T1, T2, or T3 connection. The largest ISPs all use the fastest possible connections (usually multiple T3 links), but smaller ISPs may use T1 or slower connections.

Finally, design your storefront, electronic brochures, canned messages, and other information to be as small as possible in terms of file size. Smaller files are transmitted more quickly than large files. If your storefront is filled with big graphics or your canned message runs on for twenty pages, it will take that much longer for your customers to receive the information when they request it.

Obviously, you have to strike a balance between delivering information that's vital to the business relationship and forcing the customer to wait for it. Customers typically won't be sitting around waiting for an e-mail response, for example, so you can attach a larger file to an e-mail or mailbot message than you might want to display on a Web site or an FTP storefront, where you know that the customer is actually sitting there waiting for the file to be transmitted.

26 CLARITY

Clarity means delivering information or services in an unambiguous fashion, so there's as small a barrier as possible between what you mean and what your customers understand. Barriers like this are frustrating for everyone involved, and with so much competition in cyberspace, they can force prospects to go to your competitors if they're too high.

Clarity applies to the language you use in subject lines in e-mail or discussion group messages, the messages themselves, the names of items on storefront menus, the titles of electronic publications, and the organization of your storefront. Here are some specific suggestions for improving clarity.

Avoid colloquial words or phrases. Slang phrases are often specific to a certain geographical region or a certain culture or age group. Customers in other parts of the country or the world or in other age groups may not understand them. At best, such phrases may confuse your prospects and make them feel like they're not in on the joke. At worst, they may repel people you're trying to attract.

The Net has its own language, and you can't assume that all of your customers know it. For example, the Zima malt beverage site on the Web (http://www.zima.com) has a department called "Think MUD." This means nothing to anyone who doesn't know that MUD is an acronym for Multi-User Dungeon, a type of interactive Net game.

Using words or phrases like this is like turning your presentation into a private club and then denying most of the applicants membership: those who are admitted will feel special, but you'll alienate far more people by shutting them out.

Organize menus logically. In setting up your storefront, design the home page so it tells a visitor immediately what the site is about. Typically, the menu items should move from the general to the more specific as a visitor scans them from top to bottom. For example, put departments such as What's New and About This Site at the top of the list, and leave departments like Other Related Sites and Ordering Information at or near the bottom.

Explain what's going on and what to do. Not everyone on the Net knows exactly how to navigate around a storefront or how to fill out an order form; don't assume all your visitors do. Explain how to navigate through your storefront, or use buttons or links that are self-evident, such as *Return to main directory* or *Browse catalog*. On your order form, explain how the ordering process works, how to move from one data field to the next, and how to transmit the form or clear data from it.

The best way to test the clarity of your Net messages and storefront is to invite disinterested parties to evaluate them. Ask relatives or friends to read your messages, subject lines, publications, or storefront menus and comment on their clarity and organization. Anything that confuses anyone should throw up a red flag for you.

27 BANDWIDTH

As we have said before, time is the most precious commodity on the Net, both for you and for your customers. Bandwidth is the amount of information that you can deliver or that your customers can get from you at any given moment. Guerrillas look at everything they do to maximize bandwidth at every step of the marketing process. Here are some ways to do that.

Marketing messages. The messages you use to market your company, such as classified ads and discussion group postings, should be as short as possible. A good classified ad should be no more than one screen long, a good discussion group message no more than two screens long.

Storefront design. Design your storefront, if possible, so the store name and key departments all appear on the first screen a visitor sees. Don't force visitors to wait for a large logo graphic to appear or to scroll down two or three screens to find out what the store has to offer.

Equipment. The less time you spend waiting for things to happen on the Net, the more time you have for active marketing. That means finding the fastest method of accessing the Net, such as signing up with a service provider that allows 28.8 kilobit-per-second dial-up access, getting a 28.8 kbps modem, and using a 486-based PC or better. If you spend lots of time online and you're in an area that supports it, you should consider an ISDN telephone line or a

CATV modem connection, which will give you much faster access than a telephone modem. Check with your telephone provider to find out if ISDN is available in your area; in some places, it now costs less than $50 a month for service that's four times as fast as the fastest dial-up modem.

28   MAILBOTS

Mailbots are an excellent way to improve service, because they allow you to respond almost instantly to any request for general information. A mailbot program lurks behind an e-mail address, waiting for messages to come to it. Each time a message is delivered to that e-mail address, the mailbot reads the sender's address and automatically sends a file of your choice back to the sender.

Mailbots usually accomplish their job almost instantly. It's not at all uncommon for someone to request information from a mailbot and receive it within sixty seconds. Compare that with the several hours it might take between the time someone sends you e-mail and the time you read that mail and respond to it. You can't do much better than a mailbot when it comes to satisfying a customer's request for information via e-mail.

You can get a mailbot from most Internet service providers. Typically, you'll pay $25 or $50 to set up the program and then the usual monthly e-mail account fee ($20 or so) to maintain it.

You can use a mailbot to distribute one electronic document, such as a general brochure about your company, or to deliver different documents depending on keywords contained in the messages it receives. For example, if you have a catalog, a brochure, and a newsletter sample, you could ask prospects to send your mailbot a message with the word *catalog, brochure,* or *newsletter,* depending on which of the documents they want to receive.

The server where the mailbot is set up (at your Internet service provider's location) will automatically maintain a log, a record of each message the mailbot has received. You can periodically check the log to learn the e-mail addresses of everyone who has requested information from the mailbot. If you're sending out more than one document, you can also tell which addresses have requested which documents. This information is invaluable in helping you determine which documents are the most popular and, more important, who is asking for them.

29 FOLLOW-UP

Follow-up is probably the most often neglected aspect of service. It's here that guerrillas make the difference between a one-shot sale and an ongoing relationship that means repeat business for months or years. The best way to build an ongoing relationship is through ongoing contact, a program of follow-up notices via e-mail that offer the customer more information and keep your company name fresh in her mind. Specific ways to follow up include the following approaches.

If you sold someone a product, follow up after a few months with an e-mail note offering suggestions about using or caring for it. You might also attach a list of new products you've begun offering since the original purchase.

If you sold someone a service, follow up within two weeks with a thank-you note via e-mail. Then follow up again a couple of months later and ask how things are going.

Think about creating a bimonthly or quarterly tip sheet or news update related to your products or services and e-mailing it to your previous customers. If the document contains more useful information than blatant advertising, most of your correspondents will appreciate it.

Plan a follow-up campaign before you begin your marketing attack and then record your orders or contacts by date. You can track this information in your sales order database or in a simple contact or lead-generating database you set up. (You can also use the activity log described on p. 15). All you need to track is each person's last contact date; her name and address; the status of your relationship with her (recent customer, information query, and so on); and the nature of your last contact (for example, *sent first follow-up letter* or *sent second tip sheet*).

If you've captured this activity-related information as you go along, the follow-up process is simple. Every week, select the contacts whose dates are appropriate for follow-up and then do a quick mailing.

Whenever you send out follow-up letters, however, show your respect for the person's privacy by offering to take her off the distribution list if she asks you to. If your follow-up documents are useful, you won't get many requests to stop them.

30   LOCATIONS

One of the most important aspects of service is being where your customers need you. Organizations like McDonald's, Standard Oil, and Bank of America thrive as much on their convenient locations as on the quality of their products or services. Cyberspace is a very big place, and you'll have to work hard to get the word out about your business and where it's located. You can help your effort significantly by seeking multiple locations for your messages and multiple links to your business.

Message locations include libraries where you store articles you've written, discussion groups where you participate regularly, classified ad sections where you post ads, and your online storefront.

Directory listings let you place your company name and basic marketing information for free in business directories throughout cyberspace. Visit as many online shopping malls and directory locations as you can, and take advantage of free listings wherever you find them.

Links. Many Worldwide Web site operators add value to their sites by displaying links to other useful resources. To find sites that might want to feature links to your business, use Yahoo, Lycos, EINet Galaxy, WebCrawler, InfoSeek, or another Web search engine to search for businesses that are related to, but not competitive with, your own. Visit those sites and, if they look like attractive and well maintained, contact the operators and offer to exchange links — you feature a link to their site in your "other sites" area, and they do the same in theirs. For example, if you're in the vitamin business, look for links to health, fitness, and nutrition-related sites. If you're an architect, look for links to sites offering real estate, interior design services, and remodeling.

5

Customer Comfort

THE INTERNET IS a great equalizer, where major corporations, small businesses, and charlatans all compete for attention. Without the reassurance of a physical contact, customers may be reluctant to buy from unfamiliar companies, not knowing whether those companies went into business yesterday or they've been a leader in their industry for years.

In this chapter, we'll look at nine weapons you can use to increase your customers' comfort level so they'll feel good about doing business with you. Even if you went into business yesterday, you can use them to reassure customers at each step of a transaction. Many of them aren't being used by your competitors, and most of them don't cost you a dime. Guerrillas know that properly used, these weapons help ensure that each new customer becomes a long-term customer.

31 ORDER FORM

If you operate a storefront and you have some control over how your order form looks, make it as simple, understandable, and easy to use as possible. We touched on this weapon on p. 42 in Chapter 3, but it's so important that we'll go into much more detail here. A customer who is frustrated by an order form or uncertain about how it works could easily bail out of the transaction and seek out your competition. But if you anticipate customer problems and offer reassurance during the ordering process, you'll see the customer through to a successful sale.

There are several parts of an order form, and each one can increase or decrease customer comfort.

Introduction. The top of your order form should introduce your ordering system and explain how to use it. You can't assume your customers have ever ordered anything over the Net before, so you should anticipate any problems or questions they may have and deal with them right at the top of the ordering page.

Here's an example of some text you might use at the top of an order form in a Worldwide Web storefront:

> *Welcome to the Acme Manufacturing order page. To use this form, type the correct information into the entry blanks below. You can press the Tab key to move from one blank to the next, or simply click in the blank where you want to enter information and then begin typing. No information is transmitted until you click the Send Order button at the bottom of the form, so you can correct any mistakes at any time before you send in the form. If you decide not to order, you can simply go to another Web page without sending it, or click the Clear button at the bottom of the form to wipe out any information you entered in the blanks.*
>
> *Once you send the form, we'll receive it and send you an order confirmation via e-mail so you'll know your order is being processed. Usually we process orders the same day we receive them and ship them out the following day. If an item is out of stock or shipping will otherwise be delayed, we'll let you know.*
>
> *If you don't see order entry blanks in the form below, you won't be able to order online. Instead, you can phone your order to us at 1-800-555-1124 anytime between 8 A.M. and 6 P.M. Eastern Standard Time, Monday through Saturday, or you can display our fax order form by clicking the Fax Form button. Once the fax order form is on your screen, choose the Print command from your File menu to print it out, and then fill it in and fax it to us at 508-555-5421.*
>
> *If you have any questions about our ordering process or using this form, please call us at the 800 number above and we'll be happy to help.*

This introduction helps customers understand everything in advance, removing any fear they might have about the ordering process. It explains how the order form works, and it offers two ordering alternatives if customers can't see the order form on their screens. (Notice that it even tells people exactly how to print out the fax form; most newcomers to the Web don't know anything about their browser program except how to point and click.) Finally, the introduction invites people to phone an 800 number if they have any questions or concerns. You can't get much more helpful than this.

Information blanks and buttons. Each information blank in the order form should have a label next to or below it so customers have no doubt about what information goes where. For example, rather than labeling an address blank "Address," label it "Street Address." Be as specific as possible so there's no chance of a misunderstanding. If you hope to sell to an international audience, make sure the information blanks for Zip Code read "Zip or Postal Code," since the term "Zip" is used only in the United States. Also, include a blank for country information.

The same goes for any labeled buttons on the order form. We've seen a lot of order forms with buttons labeled "Send," "Submit," and "Clear" at the bottom, with no further explanation. It's much better to label them "Send Form" or "Clear Form," so people know exactly what they do. Eliminate guesswork whenever possible.

When laying out your order form, make sure each information blank is on one line only. Don't allow an entry blank to wrap around from one line to the next, since it may confuse the customer. If your form is for a Web storefront, view it with several different browser programs to make sure it makes sense in every case. You can't assume your customers will all be using Netscape Navigator to visit your store.

Also, use all the capabilities of your storefront system to make it easier to fill in information blanks. Use pop-up menus, checkboxes, or buttons where customers can select and enter item names, colors, styles, or prices, or where they can choose shipping options. By enabling customers to click and choose items from menus, checkboxes, or buttons, you eliminate the possibility of typos.

Shipping options. Explain your method of shipping merchandise (mail, UPS, Federal Express, or otherwise). Give an estimate of delivery times for each option and make it possible for your customers to choose faster shipping methods if they're willing to pay for them. The more control you can give your customers over how their order is handled and when it will be shipped, the more comfortable they'll feel.

Costs and totals. Basic order forms can't perform automatic calculations on the Worldwide Web. Customers must make their own calculations and then enter extended costs, shipping costs, any taxes, and the total order amount. They may not understand why they have to do all this work themselves, so you should explain why. Also, reassure customers that you will check their figures when you receive the order and notify them of any errors.

Refund policy. At the bottom of your order form or on a form linked to it, explain your refund or exchange policy clearly, so customers know what to expect if they're not satisfied with their purchase. Every customer will be concerned about satisfaction until he receives the order, but explaining your policy will help set his mind at ease before he orders.

Security. Many people are concerned about ordering over the Net. Along with offering off-line ordering options, address customers' worries by explaining what really happens when they do. Here's a brief statement that does the job:

> *Many people are uncomfortable about transmitting their credit card number over the Internet because of the many reports about security problems. However, we believe that transmitting your credit card number over the Net is no riskier than letting your card out of your sight at a busy department store or restaurant. Once we receive your credit card number, we store it on a computer that is not connected to the Net, so it's safe from theft by hackers. However, if you still prefer not to send your card number over the Net, feel free to phone or fax your order to us.*

If your store uses a secure order transmission system, share the good news with your customers. Many secure server options have appeared in the past year, and if you're using one, you can offer your customers added comfort with a statement like this:

> *Your financial information is safe with us! Acme Manufacturing's Worldwide Web store uses secure server technology. The credit card number and other information you send us is encrypted to keep it safe from unauthorized use.*

Most companies design order forms to make their lives easier, not to make their customers happier. But if you keep your customers in mind when designing your ordering options, they will be grateful.

32 GUARANTEE

We briefly mentioned offering a guarantee on p. 42 in Chapter 3, but this weapon is so important that it deserves its own section. Lands' End built a very large mail-order business on quality merchandise and the slogan "Guaranteed. Period." In fact, most businesses stand behind the products they sell, but few turn that policy into a marketing weapon as well as the major mail-order firms do. These companies understand that customers are essentially buying something sight unseen, and they know that their guarantee takes the uncertainty out of the transaction.

If you're confident of your products, you have no reason not to stand behind them. A guarantee demonstrates your confidence and makes your customers more comfortable. If your products don't lend themselves to a 100 percent guarantee, you should offer a more limited guarantee, such as a thirty-day free trial or examination period.

Some shortsighted entrepreneurs think that offering a 100 percent guarantee is too risky. They're worried that they'll spend half their time dealing with returns, or that people will order an item with the idea of using it for a short time and then returning it. But not many people are this devious. Unless you're really deceiving customers about the quality or features of your products, 99 percent of them will be satisfied, and they'll appreciate your confidence.

A satisfaction guarantee should be a standard policy in your business. Guerrillas turn guarantees into weapons by making sure their customers know about them.

33 RELIABILITY

There's nothing like a little unreliability to abort a blossoming customer relationship. Customers want most of all to know that you hear what they're saying, that you respond to their concerns, and that you'll be there in the future when they have questions, comments, or more orders. Strive for rock-solid reliability in everything you do. You can build reliability in all your customer contacts at several points.

Inquiries. When a customer sends you an e-mail note asking for more information about your business, reply to it as soon as possible. We have never had a customer complain because we responded too quickly. Quick responses are most important when you exchange a series of messages with a prospect. The first quick response shows that you're paying attention, but a string of quick responses shows that you're reliable.

Order confirmation. Set up a standard order confirmation notice and send it via e-mail as soon as you receive an order. If possible, let the customer know not only that the order was received but when the product will ship and when he can expect it to arrive.

Shipping. Before you go online, plan how you will ship merchandise to customers around the world so that it will arrive reliably and in good condition. For example, you may find that you have to send items via registered mail or through an international air delivery service in order to ensure their arrival in some locations.

Follow-up. A week or two after each sale, send the customer a follow-up note via e-mail to let him know you appreciate his business. Each quarter, e-mail your customers a one- or two-page letter to tell them about new products or services you're offering or to make suggestions about using or maintaining products they've bought. Regular follow-up notes help you maintain your position in the customers' minds, and they add to the customers' confidence that your company is a solid, well-established business.

By showing customers you're on the ball, you'll combat their fear of cyberspace, and you'll make your business stand out among your less responsive competitors.

34 DELIVERY SPEED

Strive for the fastest delivery of your products or services. The more quickly your customers can receive an order, the more they'll trust you. Firms like PC Warehouse have built huge mail-order businesses by offering next-day delivery for only three dollars more on small items, and you can do the same thing.

Naturally, you'll want to explore all the overnight delivery options available to you, and you'll want to consider the various international destinations where you might have to ship merchandise. It's just not possible to ship some items cheaply and quickly to all corners of the globe. But if you ship small items, you should be able to come up with one- or two-day delivery to most places in the world at a cost that will please your customers without cutting heavily into your profits.

When you're trying to establish solid customer relationships on the Net, it's better to shave your profit a little bit in the beginning in the name of proving your speed, reliability, and professionalism. And the more quickly you can give your customers what they want, the more quickly they'll be satisfied.

35 ORDERING OPTIONS

Different customers have different preferences when it comes to ordering from a Net-based business. Guerrillas offer as many options as possible, because they don't ever want to miss out on a sale just because they didn't give the customer the right ordering choice.

For example, your Worldwide Web storefront might have an on-line order form, but some of your customers won't be comfortable using it. Having read the latest sensationalistic news report about crime on the Net, a customer may prefer to order by phone or fax rather than send the credit card number over the Net.

Your online order form should state right up front that there are other ways to order for those who don't want to trust their credit card information to cyberspace. Include your store's mailing address, fax number, an 800 number customers can call to order in the United States, and a long-distance number that overseas customers can use to place orders as well. (Many firms list only an 800 number and thereby frustrate overseas customers, for whom the number doesn't work.)

If you're really hoping to encourage Net-based orders, you can do it by offering a premium to customers who do order online. Banks offer discounts or contests to encourage their customers to trust automated teller machines; you can do the same thing to encourage ordering directly on the Net.

By offering multiple ordering options, you're empowering the customer, and having choices makes customers comfortable.

36 PAYMENT OPTIONS

Customers also have different preferences when it comes to paying for their order. As a Net merchant, you'll probably need a Visa/MasterCard merchant account with your bank, and most of your customers will pay this way. But some will be more comfortable mailing you a check, and overseas customers may have credit cards that will be more difficult for you to accept.

Everyone should accept Visa, MasterCard, and checks, but you may want to add other options, depending on where you expect most of your sales to occur. For example, if you're selling to businesses, you should accept purchase orders. If you're selling lots of merchandise in Japan, you may want to add JCB cards to the list of credit cards you accept. If your business is in Europe, you'll probably want to accept the Eurocard.

Software is now available that lets you accept and verify checks or debit cards on the Net as well. Check discussion groups, business-related classified ad areas, or forums related to small business, and you'll find a handful of merchants offering such software.

As you add new payment options, make sure your customers know about them. Each new payment option you offer should lead to a headline or banner on your storefront announcing this new payment flexibility.

37 FEEDBACK MECHANISM

The worst possible feeling for a customer is having no way to communicate with a vendor. We've all experienced this at one time or another, whether it was in a store where the manager was never available, or with a company whose phone representatives shunted us to an answering machine, or with a software firm whose technical support phone line was always busy.

Customers will never feel comfortable buying from you if they don't feel they have a way to communicate with you, to get their message heard and have it responded to quickly. Most Net businesses tend to think that e-mail handles this communications function, but simply having an e-mail address isn't enough. You or your staff should be prepared to check for feedback messages every few hours and to respond to them within one business day.

Customers must be able to learn from a casual glance at your storefront where the feedback mechanism is and how to use it. Your feedback option should be a main feature on your home page or main menu, and customers should have access to it from every screen your store displays. You might even include a brief statement about how and when you respond to feedback, like this:

> *We try hard to answer all incoming e-mail within one business day, but sometimes there aren't enough hours in the day. If you send us a feedback message and don't hear from us within a day, wait another day for a response before sending another message asking why we didn't respond more quickly. To expedite a response to your message, make sure your message's Subject line explains what your message is about; a lot of people forget to fill in the Subject line before they send a message, and that makes it more difficult to route your message to the right person for a reply.*

By promoting your feedback mechanism, you're letting customers know that you welcome their comments and questions. It improves your credibility, promotes goodwill, and ultimately improves profits.

38 NEATNESS

Neatness is a mark of professionalism that subtly influences customer attitudes. Neatness means correctness, consistency, and a tidy appearance in everything you do online. Neatness should become part of your online identity (see p. 9 in Chapter 1).

When you strive for neatness, you promote a professional, businesslike attitude. When you don't strive for neatness, customers may rightly feel that you can't be bothered with detail. Various areas of your online presence can be polished with neatness.

Text. The text you write in every brochure, storefront page, e-mail or discussion group note, or order confirmation should be absolutely correct. Stamp out spelling, grammar, and punctuation errors. Eliminate vague or ambiguous language, run-on sentences, and sentence fragments.

Formatting. Check your text and graphics for readability. Don't use graphics that are hard to decipher. Make sure any graphics you use on Web pages occur in natural places rather than breaking up important lines of text. Be consistent in your use of fonts, type sizes, heading sizes and styles, and spacing lines between blocks of text. Check any italicized or boldfaced passages in Web pages to make sure they don't make surrounding text harder to read. (For example, an italicized word may slant against a following word and make it hard to read. If so, add an extra space between the italicized word and the next word, or move the next word down to a new line.) When designing Web pages, check them on several different browsers to make sure they always look the way you want them to.

Outdated or contradictory information. When a successful company like McDonald's runs a contest or promotion, the event has both a starting and an ending date. Once the event is over, the banners or brochures advertising the promotion are immediately removed from thousands of franchise locations around the country, because they're no longer correct. When you allow information to age beyond its time, it becomes wrong or contradictory, and that's a ticket to frustration and resentment for any customer who reads it and doesn't know that it's outdated.

The online world is littered with cyber-garbage in the form of information that's no longer valid: directory listings that include the wrong URL or e-mail address, "favorite links" pages that contain links that aren't there anymore, and so on. If you've been marketing online for a while, you've undoubtedly spread around a lot of information about yourself, your company, and your products. You can't do anything about e-mail that's been sent, but you can stay current with information you've published in various locations. Every month or so, check your activity log (see p. 15 in Chapter 2), revisit the places where you've published information or added a directory listing, and make sure the information is current. If you've included any hypertext links on your Web pages or in published messages, check them on publication to make sure they work properly, and then check them periodically to make sure they're still valid. It's easy to change the name or location of a file to which a link refers and thereby render the link useless.

The disorganization and untidiness of the Net is probably its least attractive feature. By striving for neatness in all you do, you can make your company a standout.

39   PRICING

As in the mail-order business, online customers aren't particularly price-sensitive. Other factors, such as customer confidence, quality, and service, are far more important. Most people are willing to pay a fair price, and most people are willing to allow the person selling the item to make some profit. But pricing anything much too high or much too low will definitely drive business away, so it pays to consider your pricing very carefully.

All businesses want to price their goods or services at a level that generates a healthy profit, but finding exactly the right price is a real art. You want to be adequately compensated for your time and expenses plus earn a profit, but you don't want to price yourself out of the competition.

It depends on what business you're in, too. If you sell commodity items like books, CDs, computers, or office supplies, customers are relatively price-sensitive, because it's easy for them to compare prices at other stores, both online and off. But if you sell consulting services, real estate, or original oil paintings, higher prices can impart an extra cachet of quality to a product that can't easily be compared with others.

Here's how to arrive at fair prices.

Check the competition. Scour the Net and locate other businesses that are selling what you sell. If you find competitors, ask for their information and find out what they're charging. You don't have to beat everyone's price, but you do have to be somewhat competitive. You probably can't charge twice as much for the same item as someone else, but if your price isn't the lowest on the block, you'll want to stress service, quality, convenience, reliability, or selection.

Check the market conditions. Try to set a price you can live with for a long time. It's much better to set a price and stick with it than to start out high and begin dropping the price when nobody bites. If you were in the Internet services business, for example, you would know that prices for Internet connections and monthly service have been plummeting for the past couple of years. Knowing that, you would tend to price your service lower rather than higher in anticipation of further price cuts.

Constant sale prices or discounts convey a subtle image that you can't survive in business by charging what your goods or services are really worth. Sales are a drug that all too easily becomes addictive: hold a sale and business picks up; end the sale and business falls. Pretty soon, you're holding merchandise on sale all the time, just like the big department stores.

Determine your profit needs. Of course, you can't compete for very long with anyone if you're losing money on every sale. Set a reasonable profit goal that rewards you for your time, but don't get greedy. Customers seek value in their purchases, no matter what price they're paying. If they don't feel they're getting enough value, they'll go elsewhere.

The relative anonymity of the Net and the technological thrill of navigating through cyberspace don't give you the right to rip customers off. Set realistic prices and focus on delivering service and value.

6

Advertising

VISIBILITY IS CRUCIAL to your success in cyberspace, and advertising is the best way to guarantee visibility for your business. Although there were once just a few opportunities for advertising on the Net, the commercialization of cyberspace has magnified the possibilities for advertisers. With enough time, money, and determination, you can place a series of ads on the Net that will expose your business to tens of thousands of people. And with enough exposures in enough locations with enough regularity, you can beat your competitors in the battle for mind share among customers and prospects.

In this chapter, we'll look at eleven advertising weapons you can use to promote your online presence. Four of the weapons — an advertising plan, fusion marketing, directory listings and links, and brochures — cost only time and effort, and you should use them as often and as much as possible. As for the others, your budget and needs will determine what you use when.

40   AN ADVERTISING PLAN

Before you begin your advertising program, make a plan. Evaluate all the weapons in this chapter, estimate how much time and effort each one will require, set a budget for time and expenses, and then decide which weapons you'll use and how you'll use them. In some cases, you'll want to spread your budget out across a group of weapons, and in others you'll want to concentrate on just a few and use them intensively.

To arrive at a good advertising plan, consider the following:

Audience. You will naturally want to target a specific group of people with your advertising. Choose places where that specific group is likeliest to see your ad. For example, a sponsorship notice on a tightly focused mailing list discussion or a particular publication's

Web site may be much more effective at reaching your audience than a Web page buried inside an online shopping mall.

Reach. If you want to reach a fairly broad group of prospects, you will want to cast your net as wide as possible. That's when you'll look for directory listings, links on other Web sites, classified ads, and cooperative marketing arrangements with other companies.

Costs. You have only so much money to spend on paid advertising. Don't put all your eggs in one basket. In the beginning, choose a handful of different ad locations and compare the results to see which of them work the best. As your campaign continues, you'll weed out the nonperforming ad locations and put more effort into the ones that pay off.

The other cost you want to consider is time. Reposting classified ads every day requires a little bit of time, as does designing a brochure and responding to e-mail inquiries for it. Determine a realistic time budget for your advertising activities and then don't overcommit yourself when you decide which weapons to use.

Once you've come up with an advertising plan, you can execute it with confidence that it will buy you as much visibility as possible without overtaxing your resources.

41 BILLBOARDS

In cyberspace, a billboard is an advertisement for your business that you have paid for. If you use an online service like CompuServe or Prodigy, you will have noticed advertisements for various businesses that periodically appear on the screen at different locations within the service, like this:

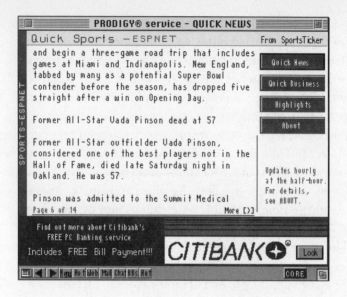

This is a billboard advertisement for Citibank on Prodigy. Prodigy billboards can pop up at the bottom of the screen in many free areas of the service. Prodigy charges $5,000 and up for a billboard like this. America Online and CompuServe also offer ads for businesses that have storefront agreements with them. Typically, a $20,000-per-year storefront agreement on CompuServe or America Online includes a specific number of random advertisements that will be seen by users of each service. These ads give you exposure to a large audience, but since they're random, you never know exactly who is seeing them.

With the growth of commercial sites on the Worldwide Web, some sites are now offering advertising space on heavily traveled pages, like this:

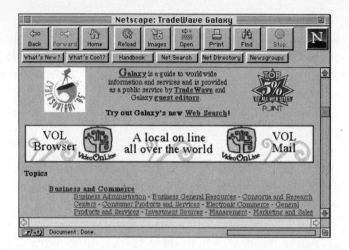

The Galaxy Web site offers one of the Web's better searching facilities as well as a directory of Web sites, so it gets a lot of use. The Video On Line company has bought a billboard on Galaxy's home page. In this case, you can click on the billboard itself and navigate directly to Video On Line's home page for more information.

You can also think of a single Worldwide Web page as a billboard. Here's one:

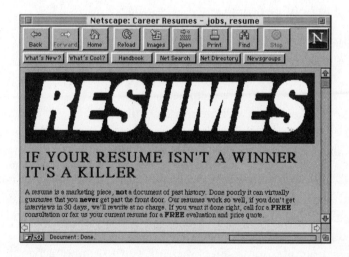

This ad for a resume service appears on the Branch Mall (http:// www.branch.com). It goes on to explain the various services offered by this company and then offers an 800 number you can call for more information. If your company has its own Web site, you might still buy an ad like this and include a link that viewers can click to navigate to your home page. Worldwide Web shopping malls like this will sell you space for an individual page that is indexed under a particular category of product or service. In some cases (as with the Internet Mall, http://www.mecklerweb.com/imall), a short text-only listing is free. In general, an individual Web page ad like the one above runs $50 or $100 per month.

If you're seriously considering buying space in a Web mall, use search engines to locate all the different malls. Many of them now specialize in a particular business or industry such as real estate or mutual fund investments, and an ad there is far more likely to be seen by a large number of hot prospects than an identical ad in a general-interest mall.

42 DIRECTORY LISTINGS AND LINKS

A directory listing is information about your business or a link to your company's Worldwide Web page that's located in an online directory. There are dozens of online directories, and listings in most of them are free. Among Worldwide Web directories and malls that accept free online listings are:

BizWeb, http://www.bizweb.com
CommerceNet, http://www.commerce.net
EInet Galaxy, http://galaxy.einet.net
Marketplace, http://marketplace.com
NetMarket, http://www.netmarket.com
The Internet Mall, http://www.mecklerweb.com/imall
Yahoo, http://www.yahoo.com

To add your listing to a directory, just navigate to the directory itself. You'll find an option to add your listing. Before you do this, though, spend a little time preparing the information you'll add and deciding how you would like it indexed in the directory.

For example, some directories ask you to supply a handful of keywords under which your listing can be indexed. If you're in the office supplies business, you might choose keywords like *stationery, office supplies, business supplies/services,* and *business equipment.* If you're adding text information rather than a link to your Web site, you'll probably get a chance to include a twenty-five- or fifty-word description of your business as part of your listing. Prepare this description in advance and get it exactly right before you go online and submit the directory listing. Show all your listing copy to associates and coworkers to get their feedback.

When your listing copy is ready, compile a list of directory sites where you want to be included. You can either add your listings to each site manually or use a submission service to add listings to dozens of sites automatically. If possible, record the directory locations and the date when you added your listings in your activity log (see p. 15 in Chapter 2), so you'll know where you placed the information when it's time to update it.

If you'd rather not spend the time to research locations for links or directory listings on your own, several services on the Net will place your link on various sites for you, and some of these are free. Two of the free ones are at http://www.netcreations.com/postmaster/index.html and http://submit-it.permalink.com/submit-it/.

Among sites that submit your links to many directories for a price is Netmart (http://www.netmart.com/hyperlink.html), which will register your links at twenty-eight different directories for $60. Netcreations (http://www.netcreations.com/postmaster/index.html) charges a one-time $500 fee to post your information in a few hundred locations, or you can buy four "keys" that allow you four repeat postings for $1,000.

Directories aren't the only places where you can establish a link to your Web site or a description of your business. You can often place information about your business for free with operators of sites related to yours. Most Worldwide Web sites feature a list of links to other interesting sites. If your business is related to but not directly competitive with other sites you know about, send an e-mail note to the site's owner and ask if he or she will exchange links with you: you agree to include a link to that site on your list of related sites, and the other site agrees to add a link to your site on its. Most Web site operators are glad to do this, because it adds value to their site.

Directory listings and links are an essential part of your Web visibility, so make sure you use them. Each time you place a link in a new location, it's like adding another doorway to your business.

43   PRINT ADVERTISING

Since print advertising appears in off-line publications, you might wonder why we consider it a weapon for online marketing. But the answer is simple: most of your online customers spend most of their time off-line! Once again, visibility is crucial to your success, and guerrillas use every possible opportunity (including print advertising) to gain visibility with their customers and prospects.

There are two ways to use print advertising to promote your online business: add your electronic contact information to an existing ad, and run new ads that specifically promote your online business.

Promoting with an existing ad

You have probably noticed that a lot of print ads now include an e-mail address or the URL of the company's Worldwide Web site along with a physical address or telephone number. Including your electronic address(es) in a general ad for your company or products is one way to boost visibility for your online presence in the off-line world. But if that's all you do, you're missing a big opportunity. Guerrillas do better.

Remember, anyone seeing your electronic address in a print advertisement probably isn't online at that moment. So along with stating your electronic address, give the reader a strong incentive to contact you online. There are a few ways to do this.

Clarify the advantages of reaching you online. Rather than having a simple line that says, *Visit our online store at http://www.store.net,* why not give prospects a specific reason to do so? Most of the print ads we see have a line like this when they could be doing much more to attract online business. For example, if your online tool catalog offers a broader selection than your print catalog, your print ad might say, *Shop at our online store for a bigger selection and more information about each tool.* If your credit union's storefront offers a mortgage loan calculator, you might say, *Instant mortgage quotes available online, day or night.*

Offer a specific incentive. If your online presence is fairly new and you're trying to boost awareness and build traffic quickly, offer a discount to online shoppers or give away a free item to the first ten, fifty, or five hundred visitors to your site.

Exclude off-line contact information. Wilson Sporting Goods ran a half-page ad in the *Wall Street Journal* for its Wilson Staff golf clubs, and the only way a customer could get further information was to navigate to an address on America Online. Essentially, Wilson was forcing readers of its ad to seek further information through an on-line address, and the company spent big bucks to find out how many people would actually do that. If you're confident that most of your prospects are already online, you can boost online inquiries in this way. However, guerrillas would also include off-line contact information, just to make sure that they weren't excluding prospects who weren't yet online.

Promoting with an online-specific ad

A surer way to draw customers to your online business is to use ads that exclusively promote that business. The other advantage to an ad like this is that you can make it very short, since its only purpose is to get people to visit your storefront or send you e-mail. And if the ad is short and sweet, it costs less, which means you can run it in more places or run it more often.

Here are a few general tips for designing an online-specific ad.

Use an attractive design. A poorly designed ad will project the wrong identity and reduce your credibility. Make sure your ad has a headline that grabs readers' attention and clearly explains the benefits of contacting you or your storefront online.

Be consistent. The key to advertising is consistency and repetition. Don't change ads every couple of weeks. Design an ad that really sells and then stick with it for a few months. It may take several weeks before you get any benefit from it, so changing it or discontinuing it too soon will short-circuit your whole effort.

Use lots of small ads rather than a few big ones. Don't spend your whole print advertising budget on a handful of expensive ads in one or two publications. It's better to buy smaller ads in several publications and to run them for a longer period of time than it is to invest everything in one or two large, one-time ads.

There's no reason why your online promotion in a print ad has to be limited to your online address. Use the ad to attract online business or explain your online advantages, and you'll get much better results.

44 STATIONERY

Most people don't think of stationery as an advertising medium, but guerrillas do. Every letter you send to prospects, customers, or suppliers is an opportunity to reinforce your company's identity in their minds. Even if most of your correspondence takes place via e-mail, you shouldn't pass up the opportunity to promote your online business whenever you send out letters via snail mail.

However, since you won't be doing much of your promotion through stationery, don't waste a lot of money producing it. Go with one of the standard designs available at any print shop for starters, and then make a few changes to bring it more into line with your company identity. And don't forget to include your URL or e-mail address.

Typically, you'll add your e-mail or other online address to the portion of your letterhead that lists your phone and fax numbers. If your online presence is new, however, call attention to it on your letterhead by printing it in slightly larger type, in boldface type, in a different color, or on a separate line with some copy that calls attention to it. For example, you might print the text *Now online!* along with an arrow that points to your online address.

The very fact that you've gone online adds to your identity as a modern business, so make sure your customers are aware of it in all your printed correspondence. What's good for your letterhead is also good for your invoices, purchase order forms, packing lists, and mailing labels.

45 BROCHURES

In the online world, a brochure is a descriptive document that you distribute electronically to people who have asked for it. Since you know you're reaching a receptive audience with your brochure, you can and should use it to go into considerable detail about your product or service. For our purposes, a brochure is a text document that is distributed via electronic mail or mailbot. It may very well be a copy of information you also present on a Worldwide Web page, but you'll want a brochure as well so you can reach people who don't have access to the Web.

The nice thing about using a brochure on the Net is that you can use it to offer details and answer questions you would otherwise have to answer via e-mail or phone, as long as you can get people to read it. To do this, advertise the brochure with a line in your e-mail or discussion group signature (see p. 23 in Chapter 3) that invites people to ask for it, like this:

Whitman Valves

143 49th St., Baltimore, MD 01298

304-555-8867 - fax: 304-555-8868

For our free electronic brochure, send e-mail to brochure@
whitvalves.com

Your signature is acceptable everywhere, so you can offer your brochure to netizens in any situation by simply mentioning it with an extra line there. You can have the brochure distributed automatically by setting up a mailbot program with your Internet service provider, or you can distribute it manually by having people request it from your personal e-mail address.

Here are a few tips about using electronic brochures.

Stick with one version. Although electronic information is very easy to change, you should come up with a brochure design and copy that will correctly describe your offering for months. It may be tempting to change your brochure frequently, but if you do you'll end up with several different versions of it floating around the Net, which may confuse your potential customers.

Avoid fancy formatting. The only file format you can assume will work with any prospect is ASCII text, so design your brochure so it looks good as a standard e-mail message. Your prospects are more interested in information than in how it looks on their screen.

Follow up the initial mailing. Anyone who asks for your brochure deserves to be on your e-mail list for at least a few months. The next time you have some news about your company, write to all brochure-requesters and tell them about it.

46 CATALOGS

Most of the nation's largest catalog retailers are already on the Net or are planning to be there. That's because it's far less expensive to present and maintain an online catalog than it is to print and mail one to people off-line. Online catalogs can offer more products, more information about each product, faster ordering, and more up-to-date information than print catalogs, and online shoppers are beginning to appreciate this.

Your online catalog should be attractive and easy to use. Here are some suggestions about how to make it so.

Organize the catalog logically. Many print catalogs are just a mishmash of products arranged from one page to the next without any particular organizational scheme. This is fine for a catalog that you can thumb through in an easy chair, but it's death to an online catalog. Your catalog should have a contents page that groups items in departments and simple navigation buttons that take people to each department quickly. If you have lots of items in each department, list them functionally or alphabetically and offer a quick way to display information about each item.

Watch graphic placement, composition, and sizes. Early online merchants often made the mistake of simply handing a printed brochure or catalog to a storefront designer and having it copied into electronic form. There are several problems with this.

A graphic that takes a microsecond to scan in print may take half a minute to download to a computer screen from the Net. Graphics may be important in selling your product, but you shouldn't make customers feel like they're wading through Jell-O to look at them. If possible, use "thumbnail" graphics that show basically what the image contains and then give customers the option to view a larger version if they're really interested.

Also, trying to include graphics in the same places as in a printed catalog can be disastrous. It's easy for the eye to follow a block of text from above a graphic to below it in a printed catalog, for example, but it's different online. When you stick a big graphic between two blocks of text in an electronic catalog, the reader may have to scroll the screen two or more times to get all the information about one product. It's much better to group all the text together and put the graphic after it.

Finally, you may want to recompose graphics that look good in print but waste space online. For example, a jeweler who shows a picture of a pendant along with the chain that holds it in a print brochure may want to crop the picture to show only the pendant in an online catalog. After all, if the pendant is the product, why waste screen space and make the image file larger to show an unimportant chain?

Avoid multiscreen descriptions. The whole point of a catalog is to offer a lot of products in a small amount of space. Using long, multiscreen descriptions of any catalog product violates this concept. Readers should be able to learn all they want to know about a particular product by looking at one screen, rather than having to scroll several times to read a windy description. In fact, your catalog should offer descriptions of two or more products on each page.

Offer a searching function. Leverage the power of the Net and the customer's computer to offer easy searching of your entire catalog. Ideally, a customer should be able to type in or click on a keyword that describes a category or type of item and then see a list of items that fall into that category, with a button she can click to view each item. For example, the Houghton Mifflin Company bookstore on the Worldwide Web (http://www.hmco.com) lets you browse among a collection of new releases, or look at titles by genre.

Don't reinvent the wheel. A quick perusal of the advertisements in the back of most online magazines will reveal at least one software package that makes it easy to create online catalogs for bulletin board systems or the Worldwide Web. Many Internet mall operators also offer one of these software packages as an incentive to their prospective tenants. Check out these catalog packages and see if they meet your needs. If so, you'll save a lot of time and energy using one of them instead of designing dozens of catalog pages and an ordering system from scratch.

The other advantage to using catalog software is that it makes ordering much easier for your customers. Most catalog software packages have a "shopping cart" system that enables users to add items to an order by clicking on a checkbox next to the item when they see it in the catalog. When the shopper is ready to send the order, the order form already shows the number, description, and price of each item added to the shopping cart, along with the total amount of the order.

47 CLASSIFIED ADS

Classified ads are a tried-and-true advertising weapon, and you can post some of them for free on the Net. They can be found in several places on online services, newsgroups, bulletin board systems, and even mailing lists. On America Online, for example, you can run all the classified ads you want at no extra cost. (CompuServe and Prodigy charge for their ads.) You can also find Internet newsgroups that are collections of ads and don't cost anything, and some new entrepreneurs out there will put your ad in a regular list of ads mailed to a specific list of subscribers.

Here are your options.

Online services. Every commercial online service has a classified ad area. You should be able to find it by searching for the words *classified ads* or by choosing an option from the service's main menu.

Newsgroups. Newsgroups such as biz.marketplace.non-computer are collections of advertisements. If possible, find a newsgroup that's composed of ads of a specific kind (computer products, travel opportunities, etc.) instead of sticking your ad into a hodgepodge of ads for every sort of product or service. Few serious buyers browse in general collections of ads like *biz.misc.*

Bulletin boards. Some bulletin board systems offer classified ads. Check an issue of *Boardwatch* magazine, check the bulletin board area of your online service, or look in the newsgroup *alt.bbs.lists* to find bulletin boards that accept classifieds.

Mailing lists. There are even some mailing lists that are collections of ads. This means people who receive the list of ads each day or week have asked to see it, which also means they're serious about shopping. One company that distributes a mailing list like this is Promo Enterprises. You can visit its Web site at http://www.webcom.com/‘promoent/ or send e-mail to message222@aol.com.

Of course, finding the location is only half the job. You must also write an effective ad to place in it. Here are some tips for doing so.

Use a catchy subject line. Your classified ad first appears to prospects as a single subject line, so make sure that subject line counts. It should identify the opportunity and entice readers to check out the whole ad.

Avoid extra capitalization or punctuation. Some classified advertisers use all capital letters, strings of asterisks, exclamation points, or dollar signs in their subject lines as a way of creating some visual differentiation from the subject lines that surround them. But there's no substitute for effective writing. Using all capitals is considered to be online shouting, and shouting at the customer is a bad way to start a business relationship. Extra punctuation marks may draw the reader's eye, but they'll also convey an amateurish impression, and nobody likes to buy from an amateur.

Write for an individual. Although your ad will be seen by hundreds or thousands of people, you should write it as if you're talking to just one person. Use language like *I, you,* and *we* rather than vague, passive phrases like *Customers like our values.* You only have a few words in which to start a relationship with the customer, so make each of them count.

Explain the offer clearly. The art of composing a classified ad is saying enough to make the prospect proceed to the next step in the sale in the fewest number of words possible.

Call for action. Tell the reader exactly what to do if he likes what he reads in the ad. It's amazing how many ads omit this simple feature. Rather than just listing your storefront or e-mail address, you should specifically tell people to call or visit there and explain why, as in *E-mail info@mailbot.com for our free brochure.*

Keep the ad visible. Classified ad areas in newsgroups, bulletin board systems, and online services age their ads very quickly. Your ad may appear at the top of its classification when you first submit it, but within a day or two it could well be pushed down the list by ads filed afterward. Ideally, your ad should be no more than two or three screens' distance from the top of the classification. If it is lower than this on the list, repost it to regain a position closer to the top.

One vendor of electronic credit-card processing software we know runs about thirty ads a week on CompuServe alone, just to maintain his visibility in a couple of key classifications. Like others who use classified advertising heavily to promote his business, this netizen knows that the key to landing at the top of a classification list on CompuServe is to submit the ad just before midnight Eastern Standard Time, which is when CompuServe posts all the new ads submitted during the previous day. If you advertise on another service, take note of how long it takes for your ad to be posted and exactly when it is posted (you might have to log on very frequently for a few days until you figure it out). By knowing the optimum time for submitting an ad, you'll always have the best chance of placing your ad at the top of a classification.

Run the ad consistently. It takes time for your visibility and credibility to develop in a classified ad area. Don't be discouraged if your e-mail box or storefront isn't jammed with inquiries or orders after your first few ads. Once you've composed an ad, it's a very simple matter to post it again and again where new browsers will see it or where regular visitors will see that you're serious.

48 DIRECT-MAIL POSTCARDS

It may seem anachronistic to use good old snail mail to promote your online business, but not when we remind you that most of your customers are off-line most of the time. A well-written postcard can command people's interest and get them to check out your company the next time they go online. For example, one interactive media designer we know sent out five hundred color postcards announcing his Web site, and in less than one week he had significantly increased traffic to the site (including visits from major firms like Compaq) and received e-mail from the president of a medium-size software company asking for a meeting!

With a postcard, you automatically overcome the barrier of getting the prospect to open an envelope, and you also save a lot on printing and postage. Besides, since the card's whole purpose is to get the reader to make an online visit, you don't need a whole letter to say what you have to say. You should be able to write an enticing message in 150 words or less.

Here are some ways you can promote your online business with a direct-mail postcard:

- Alert existing customers to your new online presence
- Announce a new online storefront
- Promote a few key advantages of buying from you online
- Publicize an online contest or promotion you're running.

The secret to effective advertising with direct-mail postcards is using both a design and copy that grab readers' attention and make them take action. On the front of the card (the side with the mailing address), use a compelling image or a compelling line of copy. If you're mailing to customers who have online connections, you may be able to tease them by simply printing your e-mail, mailbot, or other online address in big type on the front.

On the back of the postcard, write another headline that compels readers to study the copy below. Keep it short, but spell out the benefits of an online visit to your company and encourage them to make contact with you that same day. This works especially well when you have a limited-time offer, as long as the product or service you're offering has real value.

Direct-mail postcards can be had for as little as a nickel each in quantities of five thousand or more; four-color cards are about four times as much. But here's a tip: if you're running another print job at the same time, you may be able to get your printer to add your postcard layouts to the bottom of the same sheet of paper, so the postcard printing is virtually free.

49 SPONSORSHIP NOTICES

Sponsorships are an increasingly popular online marketing weapon, because they're a winning proposition for all concerned. The creators of popular Worldwide Web sites, bulletin board systems, and mailing list discussions that offer sponsorships want to earn some compensation for their labor. The companies paying for sponsorships gain exposure with a specific audience. And the people who frequent the online discussion or site find out about a company or product that's likely to arouse their interest.

Sponsorships have been around on bulletin board systems for years. Modem and BBS software makers offer big discounts to operators in exchange for a notice that the board uses their products.

But recently this practice has migrated to Internet-based mailing list discussions and Worldwide Web sites. For example, the Yahoo (http://www.yahoo.com) began as a noncommercial directory service. But because the Yahoo site draws tens of thousands of visitors every week, its operators now sell sponsorship space.

Mailing list discussions that have a large number of readers also sell sponsorships. The nice thing about sponsoring a mailing list discussion is that the discussion topic draws a specific audience and the list's owner knows exactly how many people are subscribers. One example of this is the Internet Marketing discussion (send e-mail with the subject *Info Internet-Marketing* and the text *Info Internet-Marketing* to listproc@popco.com for more information). This mailing list has more than five thousand subscribers, and companies that sell marketing-related products and services have reported excellent results from sponsorships as short as one week.

In some cases you may be able to trade products or services for a sponsorship notice, and in others you pay $250 per week and up to sponsor an active, focused Web site or discussion. But in return you get guaranteed visibility with a lot of people who are very likely to be interested in your product or service.

50 FUSION MARKETING

True guerrillas know how to stretch their marketing budgets, and fusion marketing is one of the best ways to do that. Unlike a sponsorship notice, where you trade money, goods, or services for an ad in an online location, fusion marketing involves cooperative advertising, joint promotions, or exchanges of information. By joining forces with one or more other companies, you can make your marketing dollar go a lot further.

The first step in fusion marketing is to identify potential marketing partners. In most cases, these will be people in related but noncompeting businesses. For example, if you sell credit-card processing software, you might comarket with banks or with companies that offer marketing consulting. If you sell flowers, you might comarket with companies that sell gifts, decorating services, or party supplies. A quick search of the Worldwide Web for companies in related businesses will reveal dozens of potential fusion marketing partners.

Once you've identified potential partners, there are two basic methods of fusion marketing online. One of these approaches will be right for any potential partner you approach.

Information exchanges. The simplest (and cost-free) method of fusion marketing is to exchange informational articles among related storefronts. For example, if you write an article about prolonging the life of houseplants for your flower shop site, you might interest a home decorating site in displaying that article if you display its article about decorating with houseplants.

Both articles will carry their author's name and electronic contact information. And since you're displaying yours on another storefront where visitors have similar interests, you'll attract visitors to your own storefront. The article you prepare for such exchanges should consist of a short list of tips or answers to common questions — enough to interest people and show them you know what you're talking about, but not so much that the article becomes a chore to read.

Joint advertising or promotions. This is simply getting together with one or more partners and coming up with an advertisement or promotion that benefits all of you. Major companies in the off-line world have been doing this for years — you can hardly turn on the TV without seeing a fusion commercial that involves a fast-food chain and a sports league or a motion picture, for example. In fact, once you start looking for examples of joint ads or promotions, you'll see them everywhere, and you'll get lots of ideas for fusion efforts of your own.

Fusion marketing helps you spread your company message in more places to attract more people for less money. Use it to gain big-time exposure at guerrilla prices.

7

Publicity

PUBLICITY IS the best kind of advertising, because a bona fide article in the media has more credibility than an ad you have paid for. After all, when an article in a publication says nice things about your company, you're being endorsed by a third party. A single favorable article in a magazine or newspaper can be worth more than thousands of dollars of paid advertising in the same paper. Big companies pay public relations agencies lots of money to generate favorable publicity for them, but guerrillas often do this work themselves.

However, publicity can be tricky. If you're not the person writing the article, you have no control over how your business, product, service, or news is presented. If the writer forms a negative opinion of your company, the article will reflect it. There's a saying among publicity amateurs that "any publicity is good publicity," but that's not true. Bad publicity hurts your reputation and can directly affect your bottom line. Just ask the folks at Exxon about that little oil spill a few years ago.

Unless your company is well known, most publicity starts when you contact an editor or reporter and sell her on the idea of writing an article about it. The amount of control you have over publicity depends on the specific media target you choose, the pitch you present to sell your story idea, the information you supply to support the idea, and the quality of the contact you make with the person responsible for writing the article. In this chapter, we'll look at seven weapons you can use to increase your chances of favorable publicity that will enhance your company's reputation.

51 A PUBLICITY PLAN

The best publicity programs start with a plan. You should think of publicity as an ongoing effort integral to your marketing program rather than as a one-shot effort. (You may need to read up on the other weapons in this chapter before you finalize your plan, because they're all part of it, but the plan comes first.)

There are several key elements of a good publicity plan.

A competitive analysis. Perception is everything, and the art of publicity is to create published articles or TV and radio coverage that casts your company in a favorable light. To begin, you'll want to know how your company and its competition are perceived by and presented in the media now. Study newspapers, magazines, and online publications related to your business for news of your competition and your own company to find out how each of you is being presented in the press. List every company that has been covered in one article or another (along with the name of each article's author), and then list some key messages that are being conveyed by the publicity that's been done so far.

This analysis will give you a good sense of the current publicity climate, so you'll know what has to be done to change it. And don't be discouraged if you find that companies many times the size of yours are getting all the ink: reporters love a David and Goliath matchup, if you can convince them that you're David.

Key messages. Think about how you would like to have your company presented in the media. Go back to your company mission statement or identity phrases (see pp. 4 and 9 in Chapter 1) and list some of the qualities or advantages you want reflected in media stories about your business. Think in terms of competing with other firms: cast your key messages in terms of your adversaries, such as "Higher quality than Acme Widgets," or "We're the technology innovator; Universal Doodads is the stodgy plodder." These key messages will become the real items you're selling to the media — your goal is to have them reflected in any news story about your company.

Press materials. Make a list of materials you'll distribute to members of the press and then prepare them. These will probably include a press kit and one or more press releases (see p. 93). It might also include a list of questions and answers, a comparison table that shows the advantages of your product or service over your competitors', and perhaps some photos or slides of company products or personnel. See *Press kits* on p. 96 for more information.

Publicity targets. Decide which magazines, newsletters, newspapers, and TV or radio stations you want to target as outlets for publicity about your company and then list them. And don't limit yourself to the obvious targets or major national publications. Go to a large library and research all the magazines that might cover your area of business. See *Publicity targets* on p. 99 for more information.

Story ideas. For each one of your publicity targets, craft a specific story idea, or pitch. Your publicity plan should list several story ideas that will cast your company in a favorable light, promote your online presence, and provoke the interest of editors at your target publications. See *Publicity pitches* on p. 99 for more information.

A media calendar. This is your guide to editorial opportunities at various publications. You'll use the media calendar to make sure you have prepared press materials and story ideas for a particular media target in time to have an article actually written. See *A media calendar*, below.

Your finished publicity plan will become a guide for crafting and implementing the other weapons in this chapter.

52   A MEDIA CALENDAR

Publicity doesn't happen overnight. It takes several hours to prepare and print a daily newspaper, a day or more to lay out and print a weekly, and a week or more to prepare a monthly magazine. You need to plan very carefully just when to submit story ideas and press materials so you'll have the best chance that an article will appear in the best possible edition of a publication. As you select media targets and plan to approach each of them, use a media calendar to guide you as to exactly when to make each approach.

Here's how to prepare a media calendar.

First, find out the "lead time," or the amount of advance notice, each publication needs in order to publish an article in a certain issue. You can get a publishing schedule from most publications by making a quick call to the advertising department. The schedule will state the lead time for a typical issue (and for different departments in each issue), and it alerts you to the editorial themes of upcoming issues, so you can prepare story ideas to fit in with a particular theme. For example, *Better Homes and Gardens* might be preparing an issue devoted to springtime gardening: it could be the perfect place to announce your online bulb-shopping service. Magazines like *Internet World* and *NetGuide* also plan editorial themes for different months. Once you have media calendars for each of your target publications, you can plan your attack strategy and set a schedule for pitching each story idea.

Second, work backward from the date dictated by each target's lead time to prepare a schedule for your own work, which includes writing and assembling a press kit, developing a list of references that could be used to research the article, and finding out the name, address, and phone number of the editor to whom you'll make your pitch.

Next, write lead-time deadlines on your calendar and set milestones for your own work leading up to them.

Properly prepared, a media calendar will become a daily to-do list that keeps your publicity program humming and on time. You'll have a much better chance of pitching to the right editor at the right time and of meeting any deadlines for publication.

53 PRESS RELEASES

A press release is the standard method of communication between publicity-seekers and the media. It's a document that announces news about your company and provides the impetus for many story ideas and articles. A press release has a standard format, but it's the content that determines whether or not it generates publicity.

The format is fairly simple, and you should stick with it because it's what reporters and editors expect. When it comes to content, your goal is to make what you're announcing as interesting and newsworthy as possible. Here's an example:

> **FOR IMMEDIATE RELEASE**
> Contact:
> Anna Woo
> Advantage Scholarships
> (505) 555-1122
> annaw@ascholar.com
> http://www.ascholar.com

ADVANTAGE SCHOLARSHIPS DEBUTS
ONLINE SCHOLARSHIP FINDER

Pasadena, California — January 15, 1996 — As thousands of high school seniors ponder the prospect of college next fall, Advantage Scholarships announces a Worldwide Web site where visitors can match their scholastic or sports achievements with scholarships that will fund their college dreams.

Located on the Worldwide Web at http://ascholar.com, the Advantage Scholarships Web site offers a unique search capability. Students enter a grade-point average and scholastic or sports achievements, and once the query is submitted, the site returns a list of scholarships that may be available to that student. Scholarship listings include the amount of funding, the length of the scholarship, the name of the scholarship, and the name of the college, if appropriate.

"With so many high school and college students gaining access to the Worldwide Web, we felt it was a natural extension of our service to offer a scholarship location service there," says Advantage Scholarships president Guy LeBlanc. "In just a few seconds, students can zero in on the best opportunities for college funding."

As the leading scholarship funding service in the United States, Advantage Scholarships maintains a database containing thousands of individual funding sources. Advantage Scholarships has helped students in all fifty states locate, apply for, and successfully obtain crucial college funding. Founded in 1973, Advantage Scholarships is headquartered in Pasadena, California.

# # #

This short press release starts with a release date (you can specify immediate release or a specific date in the future), information about who to contact at the company issuing the release, and a headline. Following this are a dateline with the city, state, and date the release was mailed, followed by the text of the release.

The text begins with a timely hook line (students are thinking about scholarships at this time of the year) and then presents the Web site as a solution to this common need. A press release should always answer the who, what, where, when, why, and how questions every reporter asks. Between the dateline and the first paragraph in this press release, we learn who is announcing the news, what's being announced, where the event is taking place, when it's taking place, and why it's important.

The second paragraph supplies the "how" answer. It elaborates on the news, giving more details of the specific process people will use to take advantage of the site.

The third paragraph offers quotations from the company president. Every news story and most feature articles include quotations from key people involved, so you should offer some in your press releases.

Finally, the ending paragraph is a "boilerplate" that describes the company. For this paragraph, you should come up with a brief description of your company that reinforces your key messages and can be used indefinitely. For example, rather than saying "Founded two years ago," you say, "Founded in 1994."

Most press releases wind up with a series of pound signs (#), the word *end*, or the number 30 centered below the last line of text. Any of these is newsspeak for "That's all, folks." If the release runs more than one page, the first page should have *more* at the bottom, and subsequent pages should be numbered in the upper right-hand corner.

When it comes to crafting a release, the slant you take depends on the media target you're approaching and the kind of story you hope to generate. If the release is aimed at a small local publication that doesn't have the staff to pursue and write its own articles, or if it is aimed at a magazine section that reports brief product announcements, financial results, personnel changes, and other bits of news, it may be printed verbatim. In this case, you'll make a straightforward announcement of the news. If you're announcing a product or service, you'll want to explain what it is and why it's important.

However, a press release can also be an advertisement for a longer article that will be written by a reporter at the target publication. For example, a pithy, provocative press release about how your company has leapfrogged its competition in a particular business area may prompt a feature article about how the competition in that area is heating up. Reporters and media outlets thrive on controversy and competition, so the more your release suggests these, the more attractive it will be. (If you're hoping to generate a feature article, be sure to phone the appropriate editor with a story pitch, too. See p. 99.)

In any case, make sure each release includes your key messages. Even a release announcing a new vice president can be stated to cast the whole company in a positive light. Here's a short example:

> *Phenomenal sales growth at Acme Widgets has necessitated the hiring of Janice Melnick as the new Vice President of Administration. Melnick will assume corporate administration duties formerly held by Robert Marks, Vice President of Sales, so that Marks can devote more energy to managing a growing sales staff.*

If you're getting the idea that you should create different press releases for different events, you're right. Each event you announce has its own potential for publicity, and each will need its own slant or presentation to have the best chance of seeing print.

54 PRESS KITS

A press kit is the collection of materials you present to members of the press when you give interviews, hold a press conference, or make a fairly significant company announcement (such as launching a Web site). Its purpose is to provide in one package all the basic information a reporter needs in order to write a feature article.

The contents will vary depending on what you're announcing and the target you're aiming for. Here are some items you might use in a press kit.

Cover. Most kits are presented in a folder with the company name on the outside. Inside, pockets hold documents and other materials. You can buy pocket folders at a stationery store and print a label for the outside that contains your company name, or you can spend extra money on special folders and custom printing. For major announcements, some large companies have been known to enclose press materials in briefcases, backpacks, or elaborate boxes that become gifts to the reporters or editors who attend press events, but as long as the cover is neat and does the job of holding your materials together, it's good enough.

Company backgrounder. The backgrounder is a document that explains your company and its products or services, and every press kit should have one. The backgrounder's job is to answer the key who, what, where, when, why, and how questions in reporters' minds. The specific news announcement you make at any time is covered in one or more press releases, but the backgrounder provides the information reporters need to refer to your company as they write a story.

The backgrounder is divided into several sections, including:

- an overview that describes the business opportunity your company exploits;
- a company history that explains how your company started and grew;
- a products or service section that briefly explains your company's key products or services;
- a market or competition section that positions your company against its competition and explains why you are and will continue to be successful;
- a list of key customers; and
- a management section that contains short biographies of your company's president, CEO, and other key executives.

These are the important elements of a backgrounder, but you have a lot of latitude in how to present the information. Some backgrounders contain charts, diagrams, or photos of people and products; others are all text. But as with a press release, your backgrounder should reinforce your key publicity messages.

Press release. A press release announces the main reason that you're seeking publicity at any particular time. It should be placed on top of other documents inside your press kit so it's the first thing a reporter sees. If you have more than one announcement and they aren't closely related, use separate press releases for each one. (See *Press releases* on p. 93 for more information.)

Photos or slides. If you're announcing a product, a new location, a major personnel change, or another event that would be enhanced with pictures, by all means include one or two. If you include color pictures, use slides, because they give magazine art directors the best quality and the most processing flexibility. Black-

and-white pictures can be photographs — four-by-five-inch size is fine — or line drawings.

Brochures and reprints. If you have a company brochure or reprints of a print ad or another article and you're giving the press kit to people who aren't familiar with your firm, include a copy of the brochure or reprint. Members of the press often learn about new companies or products by studying advertisements and brochures.

Competitive table. You should have provided a general market overview in your company backgrounder, but a competitive analysis highlights your strengths when compared with your competitors. It is usually a table that shows how your company's product or service compares with the competition's in specific ways. Naturally, you'll want to make your competitive table so it shows your company in the best possible light.

Press guide, or Q&A. This document anticipates the key questions a reporter might ask about your company or its announcement and then answers them. Often labeled "Key Questions and Answers" or "Press Guide," this document is a simple question-answer format, sometimes with questions in boldface, and is up to half a dozen pages long.

References. If you're announcing a product or service, include references to some of your most satisfied customers, one or more industry analysts who will comment favorably on your company, and perhaps even the names and key contacts of your major competitors. In most feature articles, reporters present an issue from more than one side. They usually obtain quotes from three or more sources. The more of those sources you provide, the more likely it is that the reporter will use them instead of digging up others who may not be so favorable to your cause.

Business card. Include a business card for the person who should be contacted for further information about the article. This information is at the top of every press release, but business cards are handy for filing.

Reporters are almost always overworked, and they often face impossible deadlines. Faced with a choice between finding information on their own and using information handed to them in a press kit, most will use the information at hand. A good press kit is your best chance of controlling what gets printed about your company. Reporters feed on information; your press kit should offer a full and satisfying meal.

55 PUBLICITY TARGETS

Publicity is a means of exposing the public to news about your online business, and it really doesn't matter where that exposure occurs as long as the news is positive and potential customers see it. Here are two tips about compiling a list of media targets.

Look beyond the obvious. You may be itching to get some coverage in *Internet World, Time, Business Week, Inc.,* or *Forbes,* but the competition for space in these publications is much stiffer than it is in smaller, regional or local publications. Most cities have a business newspaper or a newspaper with a business section, for example, and it's their job to cover local businesses. If your business is local, geography says the paper should cover it if your story is remotely interesting. The same goes for local TV and radio stations, user group newsletters, and other newsletters covering your area of business. Don't shun smaller publicity outlets; they're easier to get ink in, and they can reach important prospects.

Each target is several specific targets. Study each publication carefully and think about how its different departments or sections present information in different ways. You'll find personnel notices, company financial news, feature articles, general news or update sections, and perhaps buyer's guides or product reviews. Each section presents news differently, so each is a separate target. And each target has its own editor.

The more specifically you target your media attack, the better your chances of turning a pitch into a published article will be.

56 PUBLICITY PITCHES

Every publicity outlet is a consumer of news and ideas. Your job is to come up with news and ideas for articles that appeal to each of your publicity targets. A publicity pitch isn't the same as a press release. A press release announces a specific event, but a publicity pitch is an idea for a particular article in a particular section of a publication.

For example, you might announce that your Worldwide Web

storefront now allows people to compare insurance policies online, but you could develop several publicity pitches from that event. One pitch for a regional business newspaper might propose an article about strategies for reducing insurance costs. In this case, your on-line comparison system is just one of the solutions presented in the article. Another pitch, say for the surfboard section of *Internet World*, might propose an item about comparison shopping for financial services, listing your site as one place people should check out.

Writing a good publicity pitch is an art, but the best pitches always win. To give your publicity pitch the best chance of success, include the following:

Editorial focus. Each department in a media outlet has its own editorial focus, so make sure your pitch matches the focus of your target. Get several back issues of a target magazine and see what kinds of items are carried in your target section over time. Notice not only the subject but also the length of articles. You wouldn't want to pitch an idea that will require a feature-length article for a section that runs only one-paragraph snippets.

Timeliness. Another reason to read back issues of magazines or newspapers is to avoid pitching an idea that was done just a few issues ago. Your idea should be fresh and it should fit in with the season. For example, an article about online income tax assistance has a much better chance of being published in the January through April issues of a magazine than at other times.

Editor interest. Even if a publication's section has a stated editorial focus, you'll often find that editors and reporters have their own interests and are more likely to do stories about some subjects than others. Get to know important editors personally so you can craft pitches that will especially appeal to them. (See *Publicity contacts* below.)

Resources. If an editor becomes interested in your pitch, you can often seal the deal by offering a handful of names and phone numbers of people she can contact to complete research on the article. Many a story that had editorial interest has been abandoned because the person pitching it dropped the ball by not offering sources for quotations and further information.

Follow-up call. If your pitch gets a favorable response, follow up with the editor after a few days to offer further assistance. By doing this, you'll remind her about the story, find out whether or not it has been assigned, and get a second chance to provide input that could well end up in the article.

Properly crafted, your publicity pitches are irresistible invitations to write a story. They hook the editor with an interesting subject or angle and then make it easy to do the story by offering quotable sources or other information. A good pitch will succeed where a thousand press releases won't.

57 PUBLICITY CONTACTS

Beyond supplying the media with useful and newsworthy information, you should personally strive to become a friend of those who work there. In the face of incredible competition for press coverage, your personal relationships with members of the press will give you an important edge.

Once you've identified the key media targets you want to approach, seek out the editors of the departments you're targeting and call them, buy them coffee, take them to lunch, or visit with them at trade shows or conventions. Become more than the name at the top of a press release.

The best media contacts are friendships based on two-way exchanges of information. So when you talk to an editor, don't just treat it as an opportunity to blather on about your company. Reveal some nonbusiness details about yourself. Let the conversation range more widely than just your products, your business, or your industry. Ask the editor what she thinks about your industry, your competition, or your own company, of course, but also ask her about other subjects. You'll not only get useful intelligence about how your company stacks up, you'll begin establishing a personal relationship with that editor.

After you've made an initial contact, watch constantly for opportunities to renew it, whether or not you have some company news of your own. You don't want to overdo this and make a pest of yourself by constantly intruding in an editor's busy schedule, but you do want to make contact with important editors at least every couple of months. Include them on your guest lists for company parties. Invite them to sporting events or concerts if they have a particular interest. Call them up to ask for references to consultants or advice about some aspect of business.

Become more than a name to reporters or editors who are important to your publicity plan. You'll get more than your share of publicity, and the publicity you get will be more favorable.

8

Goodwill

GOODWILL, or the positive feelings people have about your business, is an intangible but important possession. It's so important that it's often listed as an asset with a monetary value when a business is appraised or sold. Goodwill is developed over months or years through honesty, fairness, and sincere efforts to benefit the community in which your business operates. It comes from your company's behavior toward customers and other members of your community rather than its pricing, selection, location, or other weapons.

On the Net goodwill is particularly important, because all online business is based on trust, and Goodwill involves trust. Customers must trust you to handle their transactions properly, to ship information or merchandise on time, and to deal fairly with them when they're not satisfied. As we'll see in this chapter, you can generate goodwill through your day-to-day business operations, but you can also foster it through external activities that have no direct relationship to serving customers or making sales. The following seven weapons will help you build goodwill inside and outside your business operations.

58 CREDIBILITY

Credibility, or believability, is a potent weapon on the Net because it's so difficult to come by. The physical proof of authenticity or truth that we often look for in the off-line world is missing on the Net, and we're forced to trust what we see on the screen. When you have credibility online, people believe what you say because of your track record.

Most people will take what you say at face value the first time they meet you, so credibility is a weapon everyone on the Net starts out with. But your words and actions will either increase or decrease your believability. Many people lose credibility as they conduct their business in cyberspace. Guerrillas know how to enhance it.

There are several ways to boost your online credibility.

Discussions. Online discussion groups are a good place to reinforce your credibility because they're showcases for your opinions and thoughts. In a discussion, your postings must withstand scrutiny by dozens or hundreds of readers, who will most certainly tell the world if you're full of hot air.

To make people believe you in online discussions, tell the whole truth in every posting. Avoid overblown claims and inflammatory remarks. Refrain from shouting and verbal abuse. And be sure to give others credit when you refer to their ideas, slogans, or statistics.

Publications. Every article you publish online should be clear, helpful, and correct. When you make a controversial claim, try to back it up with evidence from another source, but again, if you use information developed or previously published by others, give them full credit.

E-mail. Send e-mail only to people who have demonstrated an interest in your company. Sending mail out indiscriminately is called *spamming*; it proves your lack of concern for others and destroys your credibility.

Information requests. When someone asks you for information, make sure he gets it as quickly as possible. If you're honestly seeking new business, you'll reply within one business day. When you tell people you're looking for business and then take days or weeks to reply to them, you're demonstrating your insincerity. If for some reason you can't respond quickly, send a note saying you'll be delayed, and make sure you apologize for your tardiness when you do respond.

Orders. Fill any order you receive within twenty-four hours. If you can't do this, send the buyer an e-mail note explaining the delay and thanking him for his patience.

Most of these tactics are simple, but most people on the Net ignore them. Remember, everything you do online affects your credibility. Make sure your words and deeds enhance it.

59 REPUTATION

Your reputation is the mental image people have of you and your company. A bad reputation will turn business away, and a good reputation will keep business coming in. A good reputation is hard to get, but once you have it, it's a powerful weapon. In contrast, a bad reputation is easy to get and hard to get rid of.

When you have a reputation, people associate you with specific qualities, such as expertise, honesty, speedy service, and so on. Building a reputation starts with remembering your business mission and key identity characteristics (see pp. 4 and 9 in Chapter 1). Look over these traits carefully; they describe the kind of reputation you're aiming for in cyberspace. For example, if your mission is to offer superior customer service, then you'll want to do what it takes to earn a reputation for service.

Once you've decided what kind of reputation you'd like to enjoy, focus on demonstrating those attributes in every contact you make with the online marketplace. Make sure your employees know that your reputation is on the line during each of their contacts with customers, too. In fact, it's a good idea to write down several keywords that describe your identity or mission and post them on every employee's desk as a reminder. It's easy to get off the track and lapse into reputation-damaging behavior when you're busy, tired, or out of sorts, but a posted reminder helps you keep your reputation goals in mind.

Striving for a good reputation is like putting money in the bank: if you're doing your best most of the time, you build up goodwill that you can draw on during times when you don't live up to your identity or mission standards. And having a good reputation puts real money in the bank, too, because it helps you rise above your competitors in cyberspace.

60 CLUB/ASSOCIATION MEMBERSHIPS

Every town in America (and many cities throughout the world) has service clubs and business associations, such as a chamber of commerce, Lions Club, Rotary Club, Elks Club, and Kiwanis. These groups raise money and donate it to good causes, but they're also places where business people socialize and develop important contacts. On the Net, there are far fewer organizations like these, but they're still good places to make important contacts.

Online discussions are a particularly good place to find online organizations. Each discussion group is an informal club oriented toward a particular topic, and you might learn about a formal organization devoted to the same subject by participating in the discussion. For example, companies that develop products for publishing on the Worldwide Web would do well to join the Worldwide Web Consortium (http://www.w3.org). Another organization is the Internet Business Association (http://iba.org). You'll also find a directory of business organizations on CommerceNet (http://www.commerce.net).

Even if participating in a discussion doesn't lead to news of an official organization you could join, it may lead to informal meetings with other participants in the discussion. For example, members of discussion groups related to business uses of the Net frequently meet one another at Internet conferences and trade shows. You may be able to meet some of your online correspondents physically at your industry's trade show or conference. Personal contacts like this are important, because they reinforce the relationships you've begun online by adding faces to the names you've come to know.

As the Net matures, the number of online associations will grow. But in the meantime, don't overlook off-line associations. If your industry or profession has such an organization, joining it is a good way to gain valuable information and ideas about trends, competitors, potential employees, and business opportunities. At the same time, it gives you a chance to increase your reputation by becoming involved in a group that benefits your whole industry.

61 COMMUNITY INVOLVEMENT

Become an active member of your online community. By community, we mean people who have similar interests, whether or not they're business-related. People prefer to do business with people they know, and the best way to get to know people is by getting involved in their discussion groups, Web sites, and other venues in cyberspace. For example, your interest in scuba diving may have nothing to do with your architecture firm, but you might well make friends in a scuba diving forum who will later be customers.

The key to being involved in a community is making a contribution rather than lurking in the background. Here are some ways to contribute to your community.

Discussions. Become active in nonbusiness discussions that interest you. You can still use your business signature, so people know what you do and where to find you.

Web sites. When you see a Web site that you like, send e-mail to the owner and say so. This gives you a chance to mention what you do, which may lead to a fusion marketing arrangement (see p. 88).

Online services. Offer to help administer part of a forum, perhaps by helping to line up experts for online conferences. You'll be doing something for your online community and boosting your visibility as well.

User groups. Show people how to get online or how to navigate around the Net, or do a presentation about some topic related to the Net at a meeting, such as how to choose a modem.

Your community involvement should continue off-line as well. You might offer to do a presentation about your online business before a local college class or a community group, for example.

Offering your assistance in community affairs magnifies your visibility, because it gets you involved in a variety of activities. It also sows the seeds of goodwill by helping you establish relationships with people in a nonbusiness context. When you meet people by helping them, you have a leg up on future business.

62 PUBLIC SERVICE

Public service usually involves doing things to benefit a particular organization or individual in need. You could offer your Internet navigation services to help some group do research or publicize its cause, help publicize a fund-raiser for a particular organization or individual, help a nonprofit group design and mount a Web site or bulletin board system, or perform other useful free services.

The nice thing about public service is that it's just that: public. By stepping into the spotlight as someone who is helping a worthy group or person, you gain important visibility and enhance goodwill toward your company. Major companies establish regular programs through which employees can participate in public service, and the companies themselves make sure their name is associated with these activities. You can do the same thing, even if you're a one-person operation.

For example, if you know of a group in need and you have a Web site or other storefront, you can post a public service announcement about the group on your storefront for free. Here's an announcement that was posted on CommerceNet's home page:

> **Public Service Announcement:** Marshall Industries has requested assistance for an employee's daughter who is in need of a heart transplant. For information go to: Please Help "Baby" Meghan . . .

Announcements like this show you care about others.

When offering your company or yourself for public service, try to stick with causes that are not controversial. Don't use your Web site as a platform for a political party or religious group, for example. Doing this risks alienating people who don't hold the same beliefs, and you don't want to put up any barriers to future sales.

Guerrillas know that everything they do is marketing, and public service is a good example of this. It doesn't seem like marketing to business novices, but anything you do to build relationships with others is another weapon in the battle for profits.

63 SPONSORSHIPS

Rather than buying sponsorship notices, which are really a kind of advertisement (see p. 87), consider actually sponsoring an online or off-line event to boost your company's goodwill. Sponsorships require much more of your time than sponsorship notices, but doing the work to support a beneficial enterprise adds much more to your credibility than simply paying to stick your ad somewhere.

There are lots of opportunities to sponsor events if you're actively looking for them. Here are some ideas to get you started.

Discussions. Moderate a newsgroup, forum, or mailing list discussion. You get an opportunity to create a discussion that's focused on your area of business, and the people who participate in it know that your company is doing the work to keep the discussion going. For example, Glenn Fleishman started the Internet Marketing discussion mailing list as a much-needed way for netizens to exchange marketing information. In this case, Glenn's public service resulted in interviews in major Net-related magazines and gained credibility for his company, Point of Presence, Inc., which develops Web sites. These days the mailing list is self-supporting through sponsorship notices and contributions from its thousands of members, but Glenn's services continue to build goodwill for him and his company.

Nonbusiness storefronts. If you have a storefront devoted to your company, consider doing a second one devoted to a cause that you hold dear. For example, you might sponsor a Web site for environmental groups in a particular state or area of the country.

Off-line events. If you're located in a community with a lot of likely netizens, sponsor an off-line community event and make sure your company name and URL are posted somewhere. By donating labor, materials, or money to support an off-line event, you'll get sponsorship credit. The event can be a marathon, a bicycle race, a charity fund-raiser, a parade, or anything else, but having your company's name on the sponsorship board gives you publicity and builds goodwill. For example, one Web marketing company sponsored a sailboat race in San Diego and fielded a boat with its company name and URL on the side, and traffic on its Web site went up tenfold the following week.

64 HUMAN BONDS

People like to buy from people they know, so you should use every contact opportunity to build and strengthen the human bonds between you and your customers. Initially, customers may choose to do business with you because they like what you're selling or the price at which you're selling it, but people will only *continue* to do business with you if they're satisfied. And it's a lot easier to satisfy people when you have a strong human relationship with them. When someone likes you as a person and feels that you're treating her as a friend, that bond can transcend price, selection, service, and many other weapons your competitors may be using. You build human bonds by showing customers you care about them and by keeping that goal in mind during every single contact.

Three suggestions for building human bonds at various stages of your customer contacts follow.

Initial inquiries. When you respond to an initial inquiry, ask the person a few questions about the business she's in, how she heard about you, or how she specifically plans to use your product or service. Questions beg to be answered, and by answering your questions the prospect continues a contact that could otherwise have ended with your delivery of your initial reply. And once you get answers to the questions, you'll know more about how to help the customer and you can respond with more specific information to meet her needs.

Sales transactions. Ask the customer about other needs she might have related to the purchase she's making. You may be able to add to the sale or to steer the customer toward another vendor who can meet her other needs. Either way, the customer feels as if you're concerned about her satisfaction.

Thank-yous. After a transaction, send an e-mail note thanking the customer for her business and offering to be of help with her future needs. This shows you're interested in a long-term relationship rather than just the one sale. People like to feel important, and there's nothing like your sincere gratitude to make them feel that way.

Whatever humanity you can add to your online contacts will serve you well. It can be cold out there in cyberspace, and you can profit by making your business stand out as a beacon of warmth and friendship.

9

Free Information

FINDING AND EXCHANGING free information is the main attraction of going online. Many of the people who frequent cyberspace are information hounds, sniffing out sources of knowledge that meet their particular needs. Becoming a source of free online information is a great way to increase awareness of — and respect for — your company. Dispensing free information offers a triple marketing punch, because it lets you demonstrate your expertise, build goodwill by offering something valuable for free, and gain visibility in the process.

Like so many marketing tactics, offering free information works well if you do it right and works against you if you don't. Anyone who spends a few weeks online quickly learns to distinguish between solid, useful information and fluff. Those who offer solid information gain respect and visibility; those who offer fluff quickly fade into obscurity. So when we talk about information, we mean information that is useful to the people you would like to cultivate as customers. As we'll see, there are many weapons you can use to offer free information. Using them well will be the key to your success.

Before we look at specific information weapons, here are some points to keep in mind as you think about how you'll offer information on the Net.

You don't have to be a great writer. You can publish useful information even if you've never written anything for publication. Many of the weapons in this chapter have to do with written articles or other documents, but there are ways to offer free information that don't require a lot of writing skill.

Advertising is not information. Sending a blatant advertisement to your customer list is advertising, not offering free information. Don't confuse the two. An advertisement is an obvious attempt to sell a product or service. Its only purpose is to get the reader to buy or to request more information. Information, though, has value whether or not the reader buys anything. An advertisement might extol the virtues of a particular vacuum cleaner, for example, while an informative document might offer tips on how to use it most effectively.

Usually the distinction is a matter of content, but it can also be a matter of the context in which the information is presented. For example, Hewlett-Packard maintains a forum on CompuServe, and the libraries of that forum contain everything from user-written notes about problems with particular products, to reports of software bugs and how to work around them, to data sheets and press releases about various H-P computer products. If H-P e-mailed you a press release or a data sheet about its newest laser printer, you would consider that an advertisement; but when the press release is placed in H-P's forum library so that anyone who is interested can see it, it becomes information.

Useful information serves a particular audience. The biggest mistake in publishing is failing to serve an audience. Everything you publish should be focused clearly on serving the needs of a specific group of people. The more specific you can be, the better: you'll be more effective trying to reach a certain segment of your total market than in aiming to reach everyone in your market.

When you write for your whole market, the information must serve so many different groups of people that it's frequently of no particular use to anyone. When you write for a market segment, you give specific people specific advice. If your company sells financial consulting, for example, you might publish different documents to meet the needs of young, middle-aged, and retired investors, since each group probably has different goals. A focused document that really speaks to one of these groups is much better than a general document that doesn't. A short, focused document is also better than a lengthy document that includes sections for each group.

Information is very malleable. A lot of information is packaging; by repackaging it, you create new information. It helps to keep this in mind if you're dismayed at the potential work involved in creating a series of documents to publish. Computers make it very easy to edit one document to suit various needs, so you don't have to come up with completely original material every time. You can easily take that list of tips for winter driving safety and convert it into a list of tips for preventive winter auto maintenance, for example. Once you've completed a document, it's much easier to modify it for other uses than to come up with entirely new ones from scratch.

Choose specific publication targets. Along with writing for a particular audience, write for a particular publication location. An article you present as a tip on your Worldwide Web site might use different language from one you upload to a forum library on an online service or bulletin board system. In the latter document, for example, you might want to refer specifically to the members of a particular forum.

Check out any publication target thoroughly before you publish there to make sure it's appropriate. It's easy to scan forum libraries and then upload a document to one of them, only to find out later that you published in the wrong library. Putting a document in the wrong place means, at best, that it won't reach the right audience. At worst, improper publication damages your reputation by showing that you're an amateur or that you couldn't be bothered to do a little research before publishing.

Study your competition's information. Before you reinvent the wheel with a publication, examine related publications in the locations where you plan to publish and make sure you're not substantially repeating the information in a document someone else has published before. Frequently, reading other documents on similar topics will give you ideas about different angles you can use when writing your own documents.

Cite other information sources. You can get nearly as much credibility out of directing people to another useful source of information as you can from offering the information yourself, and it doesn't take nearly as much effort on your part. For example, you might post a discussion group notice alerting the group's members to a new Web directory, or you might steer an e-mail correspondent to a particular source of information when he asks you a question.

Get permission and give credit. If you reprint something written by someone else, be sure to contact the author or his publisher for permission. Although the Net is fairly new territory, prevailing legal opinions are that the copyright laws that hold for print also hold in cyberspace. Generally, you can get away with publishing a short quotation from someone else's work without permission, but if you find a brochure or article you like and want to offer it on your

Worldwide Web site, for example, get the proper permission. Typically, the author or publisher will grant this kind of permission for free. And when you do use reprinted material or quote someone, give the author full credit.

Log publication dates and locations. When you publish anything, use an activity log to keep track of what you published, where, and when (see p. 15 in Chapter 2). You may need to update the information later, and that will be pretty hard if you don't remember where you published it.

With these general tips in mind, then, let's look at twelve weapons you can use to offer free information online.

65   FREE ADVICE

Giving advice is the simplest and most flexible way to offer free information on the Net. You can choose whom you give it to, when to offer it, and how much detail to provide. There are many ways to offer free advice. Some opportunities will come your way during the normal course of your Net activities, but you can and should seek out others. Here are some ideas.

Discussion groups. As explained on p. 30 in Chapter 3, offering free advice in a discussion group showcases your expertise, shows your altruism, and provides visibility for your business and its Net location in the signature of everything you post. You should always look for and respond to specific questions that you spot in discussion groups if you can offer a useful answer. But as you monitor the traffic in discussion groups, you'll also find opportunities to comment on what someone else has said and give advice as you do. For example, if you're in the brokerage business and there's a general discussion about stock market trends, you could offer a synopsis of your firm's research in a particular stock category.

E-mail. If you have any sort of Net presence, you might receive e-mail containing requests for advice in your area of expertise. Answer as many of these queries as you have time to. Direct your correspondents to other sources of information to make your job easier. When they need what you're selling in the future, your correspondents will remember that you helped them.

Guest spots on forums. If you know of a forum where your expertise would be particularly useful, contact the administrator and find out about becoming a guest expert for a few days, a week, or even longer. Being a guest expert automatically adds to your reputation, and the advice you give reinforces it. Besides, as a special feature of the forum, you'll see your name and company name prominently displayed as the forum administrator promotes your appearance. (See *Conferences* on p. 116.)

A bonus to this technique is that you can sometimes gain a free account on a service where you're not normally a subscriber. For example, if a friend on CompuServe recommends you as a guest expert on one of the service's forums and the forum administrator likes the idea, you'll be given a CompuServe ID number and password to use for free for a few weeks.

"Ask Us" notices on Web sites or other storefronts. If you have an online storefront, include a department where you specifically solicit questions from visitors. You could call the department *Ask Us*, *Questions*, or even *Free Advice*. Again, the idea is to offer enough free information to demonstrate your expertise and convince visitors of your ability to help them with more involved (and profitable) projects.

Giving free advice is your best chance of showing people not only that you know your stuff but that you're willing to help. And being helpful is the beginning of most business relationships.

66   FAQS

The FAQ, or Frequently Asked Questions document, has become one of the best-known publications on the Net. An FAQ combines in one document all the common questions about a subject. FAQs came into being as a way to eliminate repetitive questions about the focus of certain newsgroups and help people troubleshoot software or hardware problems, but you can write an FAQ about anything. The idea is to create an online document that becomes *the* source of basic information about a subject.

For example, a bank or credit union might prepare a consumer loan FAQ or a mortgage FAQ. A specialty food retailer might prepare a Pâté FAQ or an Exotic Fruit FAQ. If you don't want to write an FAQ about your business, you could write one about some aspect of cyberspace, such as how and where to find information on a particular subject. There are thousands of possibilities.

To leverage your effort in preparing an FAQ document, publish it in several locations, such as your storefront, your favorite discussion forums, and one or more bulletin boards. You can also promote it in your e-mail and newsgroup signature and offer to send it to people who request it.

Most of your competitors won't spend the time to compile an FAQ, and those who do won't bother to post or promote it properly. But an FAQ is easy to create, and it can score a lot of points for your company's credibility.

67 CONFERENCES

An online conference is a chat session set up by a forum administrator on an online service or bulletin board system. It's another way to offer free advice to people who will appreciate it. But holding a conference has several added bonuses:

- you'll be promoted as an expert in advance of the event;
- the conference itself only lasts about an hour;
- you can frequently choose which questions to answer for maximum impact; and
- you'll end up with a transcript that you can edit and publish as a separate document (see p. 128).

Here are the key steps to booking yourself into an online conference and making the most of it.

Find a promising venue. Seek out forums on online services and bulletin boards that relate to your area of business and that regularly host conferences. People with business-related goods or services should approach one of the business forums on Prodigy, CompuServe, America Online, GEnie, or Delphi, for example. Each of these forums has dozens, if not hundreds, of members, and your conference may attract several dozen of them as your audience.

When you find a conference location that looks promising because of its subject, do some research. Find out where the transcripts of previous conferences are stored and look through them to determine which subjects have been covered in conferences during the past several months. You'll need to know this so you don't offer to talk on a subject that's been discussed recently.

Pitch to the forum administrator. When you've found a target, find out the name and e-mail address of the forum's administrator. You can usually discover this in a file or department inside the forum itself that explains the purpose of the forum and how to use it. Write up your conference topic and present your credentials in a brief e-mail letter to the administrator. Keep the pitch brief — two or three pages at the most.

Your credentials should abundantly demonstrate that you're a great source of information about your subject, so you'll want to present your experience and accomplishments in that particular area. For example, if you're planning to talk about UFO sightings, it would help if you can refer to other lectures or talks you've given, articles you've written, or your position as an officer of a national organization that tracks UFO sightings.

Promote the conference. If your pitch is accepted, the forum administrator will set a date and time for it and will promote it as an upcoming event. For a week or two before your conference, every member of the forum will see an announcement for it. Some forums, like the Business Strategies forum on America Online, send out regular newsletters to their members announcing upcoming conferences.

But don't leave all the promotion to a busy forum administrator; promote the conference yourself. Send e-mail to your friends and associates asking them to attend. Post a notice about the conference on related forums on the same online service or bulletin board system. And if you have a storefront on the same service or board, add an announcement to your store's home page.

Premanage the conference. The purpose of your conference is to demonstrate your expertise to a specific audience, but it's also to promote yourself and your business. A week or so before the conference, prepare a list of sample questions you feel comfortable answering, along with a short biographical sketch of yourself. Find out from the forum administrator who will be moderating the forum and send the questions and biographical document to that person.

Your biographical sketch gives the moderator the material he needs to introduce you: it should contain your company name, location, and one or two key marketing messages. The questions give the moderator a way to kick off the conference, or to jump-start it if audience questions drop off at some point.

Hold the conference. When you hold a conference, you sit at your computer or on the telephone and take questions from the conference moderator, who is collecting the questions as they're submitted by members of the audience. You and the moderator usually decide which question to answer next, and you then dictate the answer to the moderator over the phone or type it in at your computer. A conference usually lasts an hour. Because you're working through a moderator, it's a lot like having a conversation with one person — he asks a question, and you answer it.

The key to success in conferences is to try to keep your answers fairly short and to be honest if you can't answer one. It's much better to admit to not knowing something (and to offer to find out) than to bluff an answer and be caught by an astute audience member.

Promote the conference afterward. After the conference is over, use every appropriate opportunity to mention that you held it. Having held a conference automatically gives you extra credibility, and you can extend that credibility for weeks or months by referring to the event. Locate the transcript and refer people to it when they ask a question that you answered during the conference; that way, you answer their question and boost your credibility at the same time.

By chatting with a conference moderator for an hour, you can gain credibility and visibility with your audience and accomplish something that will add to your credibility for a long time afterward. Holding a conference automatically makes you an expert; all you have to do later is live up to your reputation when serving customers.

68 NEWSLETTERS AND 'ZINES

For guerrillas with strong publishing skills or resources, putting out a regular newsletter or 'zine (electronic magazine) over the Net provides ongoing visibility. The difference between a newsletter and a 'zine is the presentation: a newsletter is a text-only document that is usually distributed via e-mail to a list of subscribers, while a 'zine contains graphics and is usually displayed on a Worldwide Web site.

Either kind of publication allows you to build a community of loyal readers who are interested in information related to your business. Here's an example:

This 'zine, *i on Visual Computing*, is published quarterly by Silicon Graphics as a way to provide information and news about developments in computer graphics technology. It includes interviews with computer graphic artists, news about trends and technology, and articles about specific aspects of computer graphics, such as virtual reality. Since Silicon Graphics is in the business of selling computer graphics workstations, servers, and software, this 'zine serves three purposes:

- it provides a lot of useful information to the company's customers and prospects;
- it bolsters the company's reputation as a leader in the computer graphics field; and
- it offers another online venue where the company can showcase some of its own products.

So far, most marketing-oriented 'zines have been done by companies in the computer, software, or Internet services businesses, but that only means there's a wide-open field for you to create a 'zine of your own. A company like Silicon Graphics obviously has lots of graphics design and Web development talent at its disposal, but most of the 'zines on the Web right now are published by individuals or small groups of people. They're not nearly as graphically elegant as this example, but they still reach and retain their audiences.

If you're not up to publishing a 'zine on the Web, a newsletter can be just as effective, especially if the information you provide won't really be enhanced by graphics. Scores of electronic newsletters covering online marketing, the law, Internet happenings, and other topics are already being published regularly by Net guerrillas. Some of them are weekly or biweekly, but most are monthly, bimonthly, or quarterly.

If publishing a newsletter or 'zine sounds good to you, here are some tips to help you along the way.

Set a regular publishing schedule. Decide on the publication frequency you can live with and then stick to it. Set a realistic deadline for all articles to be finished that allows you time to format and proofread your publication, so you don't rush into print with problems. Meeting a regular publishing schedule reinforces your credibility.

Plan issues in advance. Don't wait until the eleventh hour before your deadline to decide what to write about. Plan articles in advance. Watch for bits of news you want to include in a news section and collect them as you spot them.

Promote your publication. Announce your publication in every appropriate place. This includes notifying your existing customers by e-mail (perhaps sending them a sample issue of your newsletter and then offering free subscriptions), announcing the publication in related online discussion groups, and announcing it on your storefront or Web site. If you publish a 'zine, you should also announce it in the *alt.zines* newsgroup.

Publishing a newsletter or 'zine lets you offer useful information on a regular basis, which means you have a way to maintain ongoing visibility and contact with your customers and prospects. And if you're offering value in your products and services, visibility and frequent contact will eventually lead to sales.

69 DIRECTORIES

In the online world, heaps of related information are stored helter-skelter on servers everywhere on the globe. Frequently, the biggest problem people have is finding the right information. There are a number of mega-directories at sites like Yahoo and EiNet Galaxy, but the online world sorely needs smaller, subject-specific directories. If your writing skills are limited, you can become a hero to beleaguered information hounds by publishing a useful directory.

The directory could be related to an area of your business, or it could be a public service project that you undertake just for the goodwill it creates. For example, a financial planning business might publish a directory of Worldwide Web sites that offer information about stocks, bonds, and mutual funds. One Web-based flower shop we know offers a directory of wedding-related Web sites. And if you want to take the public service route, you could prepare a directory that lists HTML programming resources, mailing list discussions having to do with adoption, humor sites on the Web, or a thousand other subjects. Either way, you can create such a directory with virtually no writing skills, especially if you follow these steps:

1. Scour the Net for resources related to your topic. Post messages in discussion groups explaining what you're doing and asking for help finding resources.
2. Create the directory and make it available via e-mail, mailbot, or a storefront.
3. Promote the directory in your e-mail and discussion group signatures and send out free samples to people on your mailing list.
4. Maintain the directory by checking the resources in it at least once a month to make sure they're still valid. (Things have a way of moving and disappearing on the Net.)

If you choose your subject wisely, your directory will be much appreciated by everyone who uses it. And that means they'll appreciate you.

70 SURVEYS

Another way to offer free information without having to write a lengthy article is to take a survey. Information hounds love surveys and statistics. If you conduct a survey on an interesting topic, the results will almost certainly attract a large audience.

For marketing guerrillas, a survey provides triple exposure.

You gain visibility by announcing the survey. When you come up with a set of survey questions, post them along with an explanation in relevant newsgroups, forums, and mailing list discussions. In posting the survey, you'll have a chance to explain who you are and why you're doing it, so you'll automatically give your business a lot of visibility in the process.

You respond to e-mail as the responses come in. As people respond to your survey, some of them will ask about or comment on your business. By responding to these comments or questions, you'll begin individual relationships with potential customers.

You publish and promote the results. When the survey is over, tabulate the results and publish them. You will naturally want to publish them in the same discussion groups where you solicited responses, but you can also publish them on your storefront. If they are surprising or newsworthy (and they should be, if you structured the survey properly), you can create a press release announcing the results and possibly generate print articles about them. Naturally, all these efforts will magnify your visibility, because your company name and contact information will be attached to them in every case.

Here are some tips for conducting an effective survey.

Use multiple choice or yes/no questions. It's much easier to tabulate responses this way. Make sure you offer enough choices to accommodate all the possible answers you'll get, even if one of the choices is "None of the above."

Make the questions clear. This may require you to break down one main question into several more specific questions, but that beats getting answers that don't mean anything. Vague questions produce vague results. For example, asking *Are you satisfied with your homeowner's insurance?* and offering a yes/no response won't tell you much about why people are happy or unhappy. It would be much better to break the question into categories of satisfaction, such as premium costs, service, and coverage.

Keep the survey short. If you can keep the survey to fewer than twenty questions, you'll be much better off. Many people won't bother to respond to a survey if it looks like it will require too much of their time.

Explain your intentions. When you post your survey and solicit responses, explain who you are, why you're doing the survey, and how you'll use the results.

Set a response deadline. Unless you're doing ongoing market research with a survey via your Worldwide Web site, set a response deadline. Allow for a few weeks in which to collect your information, and if necessary, post additional notices about your survey to remind people or alert those who may not have seen your original notice.

Make responding easy. The easier it is to answer your survey questions, the more responses you're likely to get. For example, if you have a Worldwide Web site, put up the survey there and use buttons or checkboxes to make choosing responses easier. For an example of this, check out the Mama Wants to Know department at http://www.eat.com to see how the folks at Ragu Spaghetti Sauce write a survey.

Offer a reward. You will significantly increase the response to your survey if you offer and promote a reward of some kind. For example, you could automatically enter each survey respondent in a drawing for a prize.

Survey-taking is a science, and you should study other surveys to see how questions are asked before trying one of your own. But a properly designed survey will give you a lot of marketing clout for a small amount of effort.

71 TIPS, SNIPPETS, OR NEWS SUMMARIES

Frequent tips, snippets of information, or news summaries are particularly useful ways to stay in contact with your customer base. A tip can be as short as one sentence or as long as a page or two. News summaries can consist of a page or two of short items. A snippet is simply an interesting fact, which might be one sentence or a paragraph. The main thing is to offer something useful and to do it regularly so you maintain visibility with your audience.

One way to present tips is to create a Tip of the Week department in your storefront. A feature like this lets visitors know that there's something new in your store each week (so they'll keep coming back), and it helps build a loyal readership if your tips are useful.

You can also distribute tips via e-mail or a mailbot. Offer them by subscription by adding a line to your e-mail and discussion group signatures and then distribute them each week to those who ask for them.

Another benefit of preparing weekly tips is that you can collect them. After you have a couple of months' worth of tips, you have the basis of a new document that combines the tips in different groups. Picture groups of them in documents with titles like *Ten Tips About Homework* and *Five Ways to Catch More Trout*. Each document can then be published separately in your storefront or in forum libraries, or you can offer them via e-mail. For example, you can use a collection of tips as a giveaway to entice further contact with prospects. To do this, just add a line to your signature, such as *Discover Ten Secrets of Lower Airfares. Send e-mail to me@mycompany.com.*

If you can't come up with useful tips of your own, become a collector of snippets or news items and distribute those on a regular basis. Snippets and news items make up most of the space in direct-mail newsletters distributed by businesses to their customers. Some of the facts you collect should relate to the business area you're in, but others can just be items of general interest, such as the amount of the world's ice located in Antarctica (more than 90 percent). In a collection of snippets, aim to entertain your readers as well as educate them.

You can glean facts like these from industry-specific publications, from television and radio reports, from newswires accessed via on-line services, or from general-interest newspapers and magazines. In a pinch, you can also gather interesting facts from books like *The Guinness Book of World Records, The Old Farmer's Almanac,* or one of the yearly almanacs available in libraries or bookstores.

The format and frequency of your tips, snippets, or news summaries are up to you, depending on your available time, but the goal is the same: establish a following for the information you provide and you'll maintain regular contact with your target audience.

72 BOOKS AND BOOK EXCERPTS

Writing a book and having it published is an accomplishment, and it's one of the most potent ways to enhance your reputation as an expert. Naturally, you'll want to showcase this achievement online and promote the book at the same time. Here are three ways to use a book or book excerpts to your advantage.

Publicize your accomplishment. Add a line to your e-mail and discussion group signatures that says you're the author of the book. This gives the book visibility and enhances your reputation at the same time.

Offer excerpts. Create electronic versions of key excerpts from the book and make them available through your storefront or e-mail. Offering excerpts gives people a chance to learn more about the book (which is always a prerequisite to buying it), and it demonstrates your knowledge and writing ability at the same time.

Refer to the book. Look for opportunities to refer to the book when you participate in online discussions. You don't have to stick a shameless plug into every message you post, but when the topic deals closely with something you've covered in your book, there's no harm in paraphrasing your comment with a statement like "One of the issues I explore in my book . . ." or "As I discuss in my book . . ." Naturally, you'll also include the title of the book in postings like this.

Discussion group participation is particularly effective for promoting sales of a book, because you have an audience that is already interested in your topic. When promoting in discussions, guerrillas use all the methods above in a one-two-three punch:

1. mention the book in a message you post,
2. identify yourself as the author of the book in your signature, and
3. add another line to your signature that offers free excerpts of the book via e-mail.

With this approach, you'll establish your credibility by posting a useful message, arouse interest in your book by mentioning it, and then make it easy for prospects to find out more about it by offering a free excerpt. That's a formula for success. And even if you're not particularly promoting sales of your book, having written one will still enhance your credibility.

73   ARTICLES

An article is a longer version of a tip or snippet, a fully developed explanation of a particular subject. It enables you to go into detail about your subject, zero in on a particular audience, and enhance your reputation. An article can be anywhere from a page or two to a dozen or more pages in length, and you can distribute it via e-mail, by posting it on your storefront, or by uploading it to a forum library. Once you've written an article, it becomes a long-running advertisement for your expertise and professionalism.

Of course, not everyone is a born writer, and you may lack the confidence or the time to write a long piece. But having your byline on an article is so important that you should find a way to do it. Executives at large companies know this, which is why many of them work with ghostwriters. If you don't have the time or the confidence to write an article on your own, work with a professional writer to turn your ideas into text. It may cost you a few hundred dollars, but the long-term benefits will be worth it.

When you're thinking of ideas for an article, think about how you can turn one concept into the basis for several pieces. For example, one article about passive solar architecture is good, but a series of articles about passive solar architecture for different climates is better, and it's not that much more work.

Once you've written one or more articles, here's how to get the most leverage from them.

Find a print publisher. Your article will have much more credibility if you can say that it was originally published in print, so submit it for publication to an appropriate magazine or newspaper. If it is printed, you'll be able to put a line on the electronic version that says where it originally appeared. Once readers understand that your knowledge was deemed useful enough to be published in print, they'll have more respect for you and for what you're writing. To make sure you have the right to republish your work, give only the first serial publication rights to the publisher who prints your piece. That way, the right of publication reverts to you after the article appears, and you're free to put it up on the Net.

Publish in several Net locations. An article is useless if nobody sees it. Look for forums related to your business on several different online services and upload the article to libraries in all of them. Few people belong to more than one online service, so you need to publish in several places to reach all of your audience. Most online services host forums in major categories such as business, investments, travel, leisure, and education, so you should have little trouble finding a forum on each service that's appropriate for your article. In addition to publishing in forums, add the article to your Web site and seek out other sites that might want to offer a link to your article page on the Web (see *Fusion marketing* on p. 88).

Refer people to the article. Whenever you get an e-mail query or come across a discussion group message that has something to do with the subject of your article, refer people to it. Offer to send the article to them via e-mail, or post it in a place where everyone can get it and then let people know where it is.

Writing an article is a lot of work, even if you work with a ghost-writer, but it gives you long-running credibility. Just make sure to maximize your effort by making the article easy to see and by promoting it as much as you can.

74 REPRINTS

Reprints are a way to leverage past work you or other people have done to provide information in a fresh package on the Net. Once you've spent the money or done the work to generate advertising, publicity, or a brochure, make the most of it by reprinting it electronically. Among the kinds of documents you can reprint are ads, articles, publicity, and collections.

Ads. You probably won't reproduce a four-color print ad on the Net, but you can reuse pithy ad copy or slogans in various ways. For example, you might use some of the copy developed for a print ad in your description of a product or service in an online brochure or catalog. Using the same language saves you time, and it also ensures that you're sending out a consistent message in various marketing media.

Articles. You'll want to publish your own articles on the Net, as explained above, but you might also want to reprint articles others have written. If you've read something particularly useful in a newspaper or magazine, get permission to reprint it and offer it to your customers.

Publicity. Publicity releases or articles generated from them are another way to provide information. Major companies often include recent press releases about their accomplishments on their Web sites. Even if the press release refers to something that happened six months ago, it gives readers a way to track your company's history and learn more about existing products.

Collections. Another way for nonwriters to offer useful information is to create collections or anthologies of writing from others. Publish a document that compiles recent quotations from experts in your industry on a particular topic. For example, a collection of quotations about health care costs would make a useful addition to an HMO's Web site. You could also send the collection out via e-mail to your customers and prospects.

Whatever you've written and whatever has been written about your company in the past, don't let it fade into obscurity. Keep it alive by reprinting it on the Net.

75 CONFERENCE TRANSCRIPTS

If you've held an online conference (see p. 116), a transcript of the conference session will be stored somewhere on the same online service or bulletin board system. Find out where the transcript is, have a look at it, and then turn it into an informative document. Conference transcripts have a way of collecting dust in their online archives — the archives aren't widely publicized, and only the subscribers to a certain service have access to them. You can leverage the information in them by creating a new document and publishing it in more accessible locations.

For example, you might choose the ten or twenty best questions and answers from the session and edit them into a separate FAQ document. You might also look closely at your answers to specific questions and turn each one into a longer article or tip. Once you've massaged the information into a new document, publish it where you would publish articles, FAQs, and other information discussed in this chapter.

Guerrillas know how to make the most of their time by transforming one information document into a fistful of others, or by tailoring one answer so it suits several different audiences. Conference transcripts are frequently a rich source of ideas for new documents where you can expand on the answers you gave and thereby expand your credibility.

76 COLUMN IN A PUBLICATION

One final information weapon you can use is writing a column in an established publication. Find an online newsletter or 'zine that's related to your area of business and offer to write a regular column for it. You'll gain repeated exposure for your insights and your company name, and you'll begin developing an ongoing relationship with an important audience. If the publication is located on a Web site, you'll also be able to add a convenient link to your own Web site in your byline or in the biographical note at the end of your column.

If you can't find an online publication that meets your needs, look at print publications instead. Your best chance for landing a spot as a columnist is in a publication that covers your particular industry, and most industries have them. One way to present yourself in a print publication is as the correspondent who keeps readers up to date on cyberspace developments. For example, if you're in the book business, you might become the cyberspace columnist for a bookseller's magazine. Even if you contribute a column only once a quarter, you'll still gain the repeated exposure.

As you write columns for print publications, you can leverage them by reprinting them online. You'll need permission from the publisher, of course, but online reprints help promote the publication along with promoting you, so the publisher should be amenable unless he or she is already planning an online edition.

Writing a column is even better than having an article published, because it shows that the editors of the publication think so highly of you that they'll regularly print your views. It's a great way to polish your reputation.

10

Giveaways

EVERYBODY LOVES to get something for nothing, and information isn't the only thing you can give away to enhance your visibility and reputation in cyberspace. You can give away samples of your product or service, offer free demonstrations to prove your expertise, or give away useful products that carry your company name, address, and a key marketing message into the off-line world.

When you give things away, you're demonstrating your confidence. In turn, customers feel confident about buying from you, so they do. Confidence is a precious commodity in cyberspace, and giveaways are an important way to engender it.

Giveaways can also shorten the time between when customers first learn of your product and when they decide to buy it. In effect, you make customers aware of the product and let them see or try it at the same time. In this chapter, we'll look at five specific weapons you can use to build confidence through giveaways, but first, here are some tips about conducting a giveaway on the Net.

Promote your offer. Nobody will want what you're offering if nobody knows about it. Promote your giveaway in your e-mail and discussion group signatures, in your storefront, and in newsgroups that contain notices about free items, such as *alt.consumers.free-stuff* or *biz.marketplace.non-computer.*

Offer something relevant and valuable. Most people will take giveaway items if they're even remotely interested in them, but offering useless items or items that don't reflect well on your business is a mistake. Your giveaway should be an advertisement for your business or a sample of your product. And it should be something useful by itself. Deliver as much value as you can with your giveaways, or else they'll promote your stinginess or lack of professionalism.

Deliver it promptly. When someone is interested in your free item, deliver it as quickly as possible. For example, software makers offer free samples of their programs on Web sites and FTP sites. When someone wants a copy of the sample, she can download it immediately. If your giveaway is a text document, consider offering it via a mailbot, so that it can be delivered instantly.

Follow up. If you have the e-mail addresses of people who have requested your giveaway (and you will if you use e-mail or a mailbot as the distribution mechanism), send follow-up notes a few days later to ask if the customers have any questions about your offer. In the chaos of the Net, people can easily request a document, read it, and then forget about it. By following up, you can often turn shoppers into buyers.

Giveaways work for food, soap, perfume, and other tangible goods, but making them work for any business is simply a matter of packaging what you sell as something that you can offer as a sample or demonstration. The weapons below will help you find a way to use the giveaway tactic no matter what your business is.

77 SAMPLES

Free samples are one of the oldest, most effective, and most used marketing weapons for consumer products companies. When you have confidence in your product, there's no better way to attract buyers than to let them see and try it. You can use your online connection to offer and in some cases distribute samples of your products.

Most of us think of free samples as those little bottles of mouthwash or tubes of toothpaste that come in the mail, but you don't have to be in a consumer products business to offer samples. Netscape Corporation became the world leader in Worldwide Web browser software by giving away copies of its program, and you can find everything from computer games to network utility programs offered as samples on the Net.

Even if you can't distribute your sample electronically, you can offer it that way. By posting your sample offer in your e-mail and discussion group signatures, on your Web site or other storefront, and in relevant discussion groups, you qualify your prospects. Rather than giving a sample to everyone, post notices only in certain discussions to focus on a particular market. When people respond, you'll know they're likely customers for your product.

If your product has mass appeal, you can post notices in newsgroups like *alt.consumer.free-stuff* to cast your net wide. SmithKline Beecham did this to offer samples of its Aquafresh whitening toothpaste and got hundreds of responses.

If you're in an information-based business, give away written samples of your work. You can give away articles or tip sheets that demonstrate your knowledge of specific subjects (see Chapter 9 for a list of information-based weapons you might offer) or offer samples of financial plans, travel itineraries, structural analyses, or other documents you've prepared for previous clients.

Providing something free is an easy way to get customers interested in your company. The key to making samples work is offering the right samples to the right audience. Properly planned, a sample giveaway should bring big results without costing you much time or money.

78 DEMONSTRATIONS

Samples work best for products people can easily use or understand by themselves. Demonstrations, in contrast, let you show people what you can do for them or let you show what a more complex product can do. Computer makers, power tool companies, vacuum cleaner makers, and many other industries use demonstrations to prove their products' worth, and you can too.

Net-based demonstrations have to be something you can deliver electronically. If you take a quick look around the Web, you'll see demonstrations of virtual reality software, sound software, Internet conferencing systems, and other technological products, but this is only the beginning. If you're in an information-based business such as insurance, financial counseling, law, or scholarship funding, you can offer free samples of your work by delivering a useful document that helps customers and shows what you know. Here are some ways to demonstrate your expertise on the Net.

Evaluations. A free analysis or evaluation of the customer's needs is one attractive sample you can offer. Auto repair shops often offer free safety checks, for example, and you can come up with a way to offer a quick evaluation of someone's insurance needs, investment options, and so on. If you're in the publicity business, you could prepare a brief analysis of publicity options for each prospect. A financial planner might offer a quick portfolio analysis. An advertising agency might offer a media analysis or some sample ad copy.

To standardize this procedure so you don't spend too much time on each analysis, prepare a short questionnaire for prospects to get a little information about their business and ask them to fill it out and send it to you first. Once you receive the answers, you can complete a standard analysis form with answers tailored to each prospect.

E-mail consulting. Offer a free consultation limited to a page or two of e-mail. One or two pages is plenty of space to show a prospect what you can do. Ask prospects to send you up to five questions or statements of needs and offer to answer or evaluate them for free.

Phone consulting. You can also offer a specific amount of telephone consulting for free. Offer five, ten, or fifteen free minutes to demonstrate what you know and how you can help.

There's nothing like a demonstration to help prospects visualize themselves using your product or service. Once you get people to request a demonstration, you're three quarters of the way to making the sale.

79 SOFTWARE

If there's one thing you can be sure about when you're marketing online, it's that your audience uses computers and software. That's why free software is a natural giveaway item for the Net. You'll notice lots of software companies giving away free copies of their programs, but in this case we're talking about your company's giving away a useful piece of software that displays your company's name.

Large corporations often customize screen saver programs to display their corporate logo or company name, but you don't have to be in the Fortune 1000 to obtain custom software of your own. Big companies have in-house programming staffs to handle software customization projects, but you can find other ways to put your name up on customers' screens on a regular basis.

The keys to inexpensive software are shareware and freeware. These kinds of software are usually developed by individuals and distributed for free in online libraries or via user groups. Freeware can be used for free; shareware authors ask users to send in a small registration fee if they find the program useful. Either way, you can scout out interesting or useful programs and then contact the author about customizing it to display your company name. You should be able to find an author who will do the job for a few hundred dollars.

You can distribute software like this right over the Net if you have a Web site, an FTP site, or another storefront, but you'll get more customer contact if you distribute it on a floppy disk. This way, customers have to ask for the software (which increases the chances that you'll find people who really want it), and you get to mail out a diskette with a custom label containing your company name, along with a letter or brochure describing your products or services.

Among the types of software you might give away are the following:

Screen savers — These can flash your company name, logo, or slogan on the screen.

Games — Find a good shareware or freeware game and give it away. If you get the author to add your company name to the game's startup screen and the game is highly addictive, you'll get a lot of exposure.

Utilities — Giving away a utility program is the software equivalent of handing out Swiss Army knives. If a useful utility has your company name on its startup screen, customers will be reminded of you each time they use it.

To increase your visibility, collect a group of utilities that all relate to a specific computer function and then distribute them on a disk with a custom label as a collection with your company's name, as in *The Acme Disk Utility Collection* or *The Superior Graphics Utility Toolkit.* You'll get more promotional mileage out of a utility collection if you can find ones that have something to do with your business. For example, a credit union might distribute a collection containing a mortgage calculator, a college savings template, a net worth template, and a portfolio analyzer. This way, customers will be involved in an activity related to your business each time they use the software.

Computers and software go hand in hand, but guerrillas know

how to leverage this combination to build customer gratitude and market visibility.

80 ADVERTISING SPECIALTIES

Ad specialties are free gifts that you give to customers or prospects in thanks for their interest or their business. A quick look in the Yellow Pages will reveal several companies in the advertising specialties business. There are pens, pencils, scratch pads, clocks, lighters, shirts, hats, aprons, coffee mugs, coasters, letter openers, rulers, tape measures, watches, magnifying glasses, and hundreds of other items to choose from, and most of them usually look and feel much more expensive than they really are. For example, you can get nice-looking ballpoint pens imprinted with your company name and logo for just a few cents apiece. Each time you give one of these items away, it increases your company's visibility while generating a sense of gratitude and obligation in the recipient.

To promote your online business, look for items that will be useful at a desk or near a computer. You might give away diskette holders, screen cleaning kits, or disk drive cleaning kits, for example. This way, the recipient is more likely to use the item when she is in a position to visit your storefront or contact your online business.

But even if you give away unrelated items, you can be sure they'll be appreciated. Here are some more tips for buying and using ad specialties.

Buy small quantities at first. If you haven't given away items before, buy in the smallest possible quantity to test the water. If your giveaway proves a hit, you can always order more.

Give things away as a promotion. Mail-order firms and magazines frequently offer free gifts for the first order or subscription, and you can too. Mention the free gift in your advertisements or use it as the reason for a special event. For example, if you buy T-shirts to give away, hold a T-shirt sale to generate excitement.

Advertising specialties will never carry a lot of your marketing load, but they can help add value to your offerings, improve goodwill, and increase customer satisfaction. If you're in a hotly contested market and you're already using many other weapons, ad specialties might give you the edge you need.

81   COUPONS

Coupons are another powerful and often-used weapon in the consumer products marketing wars, but guerrillas increasingly use them to boost sales in a wide variety of businesses. Distributing coupons increases visibility for your company and your product and offers a powerful incentive to buy.

Coupons work best when you're using the online market to promote sales in your off-line business, and they're a good way to try out online promotion before leaping into your own storefront. For example, Tower Records used the Net to distribute a coupon offering a two-dollar discount on some of its music soundtrack CDs via the Worldwide Web. The coupon was presented on CouponNet, a central location for coupons on the Net, and customers could print it out and take it to a Tower Records store for the discount.

Used this way, coupons increase traffic to your store, spark sales of both the discounted item and others, and give your company visibility in cyberspace at the same time. To learn more about CouponNet, visit the site at http://www.couponnet.com.

11

Special Events

S PECIAL EVENTS ARE a sure-fire way to attract extra attention to your business. They create an atmosphere of excitement that draws both new and old customers, and they give you extra publicity exposure in the off-line world as well as in cyberspace.

Anything you do outside the normal operation of your business can be turned into a special event, whether it's a series of classes, a grand opening or reopening, a contest, or a celebrity appearance. But whatever the event, the keys to success are planning and promotion.

Planning. Some companies plan special events months or even years in advance, especially if the event is tied in with some future occasion, like the next Olympics. With proper planning, you can:

- choose the best possible time for the event, perhaps timing it to coincide with an annual show, conference, or holiday;
- line up celebrities or experts whose schedules are booked far in advance;
- think through the whole event to prepare for every contingency and deliver the most excitement and value to your customers; and
- map out a publicity campaign that will boost awareness and attendance.

Promotion. Special events aren't very special if nobody attends them. The whole point of a special event is to generate publicity and bring people to your business. The special event is the news hook in press releases you send out, so the more unusual or amazing it is, the better your chances are of turning it into a news story.

For example, a garden-variety grand opening for your online jewelry store probably won't make the pages of *Internet World*, but it might if you gave away uncut diamonds to the first ten visitors. If you're seeking local media exposure for a new bulletin board system, you might co-promote the grand opening with a local radio or TV station by featuring one of the station's personalities as your online guest.

Along with publicity, you should promote your special event in every way you can. For example:

- Take out classified ads announcing it on appropriate bulletin boards, newsgroups, and online services.
- Post announcements about the event in discussion groups related to your business. (Many discussion groups prohibit blatant advertisements, but an announcement about an event isn't an ad, so it should be welcome.)
- Place radio or TV ads in your local area if you're promoting a bulletin board's grand opening.
- Remind customers of the upcoming event at every contact, whether you're making a sale or just answering questions.
- Announce the upcoming event on the front page of your storefront or Web site.
- Add a notice about the event to your e-mail and discussion group signatures.

If you plan your event well in advance, you'll be able to find the best places to promote it. Once you locate your promotion targets, begin promoting several weeks before the event to ensure a good audience.

Special events can bring people to your online storefront, but even if you operate from an e-mail box, they increase awareness of and demand for your services. In this chapter, we'll look at four specific weapons you can use in special events. We cover each weapon separately, but there's no reason why you can't combine them for greater impact. For example, your grand opening might feature a contest and a celebrity appearance, or you might host a celebrity author and include a contest in which the prize is signed copies of the author's book. Once you begin looking for special events marketing opportunities, you'll come up with lots of ideas of your own for ways to make them truly special.

82 SEMINARS AND WORKSHOPS

A seminar or workshop series adds a new dimension to your business by educating customers and prospects. You can explain specific aspects of your business or offer advice about buying or using the products you sell. For example, appliance shops often hold cooking classes, and camera shops offer photography or videography lessons. Events like this give customers a solid, noncommercial reason for visiting your business. And once you attract people for a class, they often buy merchandise from you so they can implement what they've learned.

A seminar is one session, but there's nothing to stop you from holding a series of workshops and spreading them out over several weeks. With one new lesson a week, you'll create a loyal following for a longer period of time.

In the off-line world, you would conduct the seminar or workshop series in your physical store. In the online world, you can deliver a one-time seminar or a series of weekly lessons via your storefront or electronic mail. Conduct the seminar by distributing written documents and taking questions via e-mail, or use a chat session or conferencing facility. For example, you can rent a chat room at Peachweb (http://www.peachweb.com) and then direct attendees there for question/answer sessions at a specific time, or you can simply offer to answer questions via e-mail. You can even set up a message board on your Web site or bulletin board and invite attendees to post questions there.

Whichever Net technology you use to deliver an online seminar or workshop, here are four tips about how to conduct it.

Deliver the information in easily digestible chunks. Offer each seminar or workshop segment in a document that can be read completely in fifteen minutes or less. Remember that you're delivering all the information in writing, so use lots of examples and write clearly to make sure your audience will understand you.

Answer questions during a specific time of day for a limited time. Answering questions is part of the seminar process, so make yourself available to do so after each session. At the top of each seminar document, announce that you'll answer questions for a specific length of time, say for a day or two following each seminar or lesson. Suggest that attendees copy the portion of your lesson that they have a question about and e-mail it to you with their question. Try to answer every question you receive within twenty-four hours.

Compile multiple segments into a longer document. After the seminar is over, edit all the workshop segments into a longer document and publish it separately. This way, you leverage the work you did on the seminar by creating an article or booklet that will continue to help new customers on the Net for months or years to come. (See Chapter 9.)

Spark interest with a contest or celebrity appearance. Increase attendance at your online seminars or workshops by having a celebrity guest lecturer during one session or by holding a contest for those who attend. (See *Contests*, p. 142, and *Celebrity appearances*, p. 143.)

By hosting a seminar or a series of workshop sessions, you help your customers learn more, build goodwill, boost your credibility and reputation, attract new business, and increase your company's visibility. Whether you host a one-time seminar or a workshop series that spans several weeks, you'll have a powerful weapon for making your business stand out in the crowd.

83   GRAND OPENINGS

Every business deserves a grand opening, and online businesses are no exception. Whether you're operating out of an e-mail address or you've spent months designing a fancy storefront, a grand opening gives you a reason to issue a press release, to invite people to check out your company, and to offer visitors a reward that will start your business relationship off on the right foot.

Most businesses operate for several weeks before holding a grand opening. What puts the "grand" in grand opening is the atmosphere of excitement that surrounds it. Physical stores use special signs, balloons, searchlights, entertainers, publicity, and other weapons to create an atmosphere of excitement. Visitors attend a grand opening because they'll be entertained, meet celebrities, win special prizes, get free food or drinks, or otherwise gain something that they wouldn't get if they visited the store on any other day.

When you boil it all down, a grand opening has three key requirements for success:

- special attractions not normally available;
- a time limit that brings people to your business on a certain day or days; and
- an aura of excitement.

These are the three qualities to seek when you hold a grand opening for your online business. You may not be able to pass out hot dogs at your electronic storefront, but there are many ways to meet the three crucial grand opening requirements. Let's take one requirement at a time.

Special attractions. The best kinds of special attractions are ones that bring people to your business and promote the business at the same time. If you're in a service business such as engineering, investments, accounting, or publicity, for example, offer customized samples of a portion of your service on the day of the grand opening — a quickie portfolio analysis, for example. (See *Samples* on p. 131 for more information.) If you're selling products, offer free ones to the first fifty visitors to your storefront or to the first fifty people who contact you via e-mail. You can also offer special discounts on products or services.

Time limit. In the off-line world, few grand openings last more than a few days, because it costs too much to rent all those searchlights and other special events items for longer than that. When you're online, however, you can extend your grand opening over two weeks or even a month. You don't want it to last forever, but it should last long enough for you to get the word out about it. Even a one-month grand opening isn't too long to introduce netizens around the world to your online storefront.

Excitement. Much of your grand opening's excitement will come from the quality of the special attractions you offer and the amount of publicity you generate. But there are other ways to create excitement, such as using blinking text, graphics, sound, or video in your storefront. Try to engage visitors as much as possible. Ask for comments on each page of your new storefront, or lead people on a tour by including on every page a clue to a puzzle they can solve to win a prize. Ideally, your event should encourage visitors to check out every nook and cranny of your storefront or to read every piece of descriptive or promotional literature about your business.

If your grand opening meets the three key requirements and you promote it properly in advance, it will attract new and old customers, create goodwill, and boost sales over the long term.

84 CONTESTS

Contests automatically generate excitement about your company, because everyone likes to be a winner. A well-designed contest will increase traffic to your online business, improve off-line and on-line visibility, increase sales, and leave your customers feeling good whether they win or not. Contests work so well that you see them on dozens of Web sites now, and most online services have been hosting several contests at once for years. For a sampling of what people are giving away, search for contests at the Yahoo site (www.yahoo.com). You'll find dozens of lotteries, giveaways, pools, and contests requiring submissions. You'll also get lots of ideas about how to structure a contest of your own.

Here are some ideas for holding a good contest.

Offer something worth winning. Interest in a contest is directly proportional to the value of the prize. No matter how astronomical the odds, millions of people enter the Publisher's Clearing House sweepstakes because any chance at winning millions of dollars is worth taking. A significant prize may not cost you much if you give away something related to your business — airline companies give away frequent flyer miles, for example. But even if you have to go out and buy a prize, the traffic you generate will be worth it.

Select the audience by selecting the prize. While you want to offer an attractive prize, choose one that appeals to the right people. If you give away money, a car, or a trip to Hawaii, you'll attract everyone on the Net, including preteenagers. By choosing a prize that relates directly to your business, you'll attract only potential customers.

Offer consolation prizes. The grand prize is what will make people want to enter your contest, but consolation prizes make the contest look more winnable. Everyone is trying for the big prize, but knowing that there are other prizes makes people think that they're more likely to get lucky. In fact, you might offer an inexpensive prize to everyone who enters.

Think globally. When offering prizes, don't forget that the Net is an international medium. You may have a winner who lives halfway around the world, and you wouldn't want to disqualify someone because of who she is or where she lives. Also, make sure the item you give away can be delivered easily to any potential winner.

Know the rules. Make sure that there are no legal restrictions on awarding your prize to whoever might win it. Some states place restrictions on who can win certain goods in a contest. For some basic information about contest law in the United States, look at the short article on the subject at the Advertising Law Internet site at http://www.webcom.com/~lewrose/home.html.

You can hold contests at any time and for any reason, whether it's launching your new business, reviving interest after a few months, or keeping visitors returning month after month to compete for a new prize. However and whenever you hold a contest, though, there's nothing like it for attracting people to your business.

85 CELEBRITY APPEARANCES

Online services use celebrity appearances every day to keep their subscribers interested and connected. Essentially, hosting a celebrity appearance leverages the celebrity's fame so that your company basks in the glow of that fame for a short time. Customers appreciate your giving them access to the celebrity, and many of them discover your company in the process.

On online services, celebrities appear daily in conferences and chat sessions. But you can host a celebrity simply by getting one to agree to respond to e-mail submitted via your mailbox or storefront. This is much more convenient for the celebrity, since it doesn't require him or her to be in a specific place at a particular time (as a chat session does), but it has the same promotional value.

To gain maximum leverage from a celebrity appearance, choose someone whose claim to fame has something to do with your business. This gives you a double benefit: you attract people because of the celebrity's fame, and the celebrity's appearance is a tacit endorsement of your company. For example, if you were in the investment counseling business and you hosted an appearance by the author Charles J. Givens, your customers would assume that Mr. Givens approved of your investment counsel. You would get the same double bonus for an online therapy hotline if you could convince M. Scott Peck, Gail Sheehy, or another famous self-help author to appear for you.

Celebrities often donate their time for charitable causes, but they may want compensation for appearing at your business, even if it's only an online appearance. This really depends on their level of fame and whether or not they feel the appearance is of benefit to them. To ensure that the appearance does benefit the celebrity you choose, find someone with a book or another item to sell and offer to sell or give away copies. This way, the celebrity gains extra publicity and you gain a way to attract customers.

Celebrity appearances add excitement and appeal to your business. By themselves, they give people a good reason to visit your business, and when combined with a contest or grand opening, they double or triple the drawing power of your event.

12

Referrals

REFERRALS ARE the easiest and least expensive way to market your business. It's much simpler and cheaper to develop repeat sales to a group of satisfied customers you've developed over the years than to find new customers. Also, satisfied customers are your best salespeople, because they spread the word about your quality, value, and service to their friends. And when people tell their friends about a good value, the friends tend to listen.

Referral marketing is no secret. Magazines, mail-order firms, book and music clubs, and online services are only a few of the businesses that routinely offer rewards to existing customers for referring new ones. One of the most dramatic examples was MCI's Friends & Family promotion, where customers got extra long-distance phone discounts by signing up their friends with MCI. The promotion created such a surge in MCI's market share that it took years for Sprint and AT&T to recover.

Referrals incorporate high-leverage weapons for increasing your online sales, but that leverage cuts both ways. The same customer who can sing your praises can also broadcast your failings. In the off-line world, one person's bad experience with a business is conveyed personally to an average of twenty-two other people. In the online world it's much worse, because your disgruntled customers can broadcast their dissatisfaction at discussion groups frequented by hundreds or thousands of people.

That's why referral weapons are the part of your arsenal that you'll want to hold back until you're sure your business is delivering the kind of value and service that will deserve your customers' praise. Every business has an occasional customer who won't be satisfied no matter what, but before you seek referrals, your business should be a well-oiled satisfaction machine that creates ninety-nine deliriously happy customers for every unhappy one.

With that in mind, let's look at four referral weapons.

86   GIFT CERTIFICATES

Gift certificates are offers of free gifts or discounts to the bearer. We think of these as pieces of paper that offer a one-time reward, but you can expand the concept in the online world to generate much bigger results. Gift certificates are one of the most popular weapons new businesses use to attract customers, because everyone likes a discount. Assuming you're offering something people want, most of them will give your business a try on the strength of a gift certificate alone.

There are several ways to use gift certificates to attract customers both old and new. Here are several ideas.

Referring businesses. Find other online businesses that are in a strong position to refer customers to you and give those businesses free or discounted products or services for each new customer they refer. For example, Web site operators offer free storage space and design services to marketing consultants who bring them new customers. Florists offer free arrangements to interior design firms that recommend them. Online CD stores offer free music selections to stereo or home theater vendors who recommend them. Speakers offer to present their program for free to meeting planners or speakers' agents who recommend them to other meeting planners. The possibilities of such exchanges are endless, and they benefit everyone concerned.

Repeat customer bonuses. If you're selling products, include a gift certificate for a discount on the next purchase inside the box you ship to the customer. This immediately gets the customer thinking about the next purchase, and it does that at the best possible time: when he is pleased at having received your merchandise. This tactic works best, of course, when you've delivered the item promptly. Instead of gift certificates, many businesses use frequent-buyer clubs or punch cards that offer a substantial free gift after the person has made half a dozen or more purchases. It's easy to track repeat sales on a computer to create your own frequent buyer club.

Referral bonuses. It's nice to be grateful when a current customer refers a new one, but it's better to put your money where your sentiments are. Offer gift certificates or discounts to your customers in exchange for new customer referrals. Let customers know about this program as soon as they make their first purchase. If they're happy with your service or merchandise, they'll use referrals to save money on their next purchase.

Gifts that bring new customers. If your customers are truly satisfied with you, they may want to introduce their friends to your business by way of a gift. Most off-line businesses sell gift certificates to their customers for use as gifts, and you should too. A gift certificate like this is practically a guarantee of a new customer. Many businesses wait until Christmas to promote their gift certificates, but guerrillas promote them all year long, for birthdays, anniversaries, weddings, Valentine's Day, and other occasions.

To make your gift certificates really move, offer the buyer an extra incentive for giving them. Give buyers a discount on their next purchase, for example. Mail-order firms like Harry & David use this technique very effectively to increase the number of gifts their customers buy for others: right on Harry & David's holiday order form, there's a space to choose a gift for yourself at a discount.

As you can see, there are plenty of ways to use gift certificates to increase your sales. But the online world creates some challenges when it comes to actually delivering gift certificates. Any electronic certificate can be easily duplicated, so you'll want to protect your business by delivering certificates in such a way that they can be used only by the intended person. Usually this means assigning a unique code number to each certificate.

Here are four ways to distribute gift certificates for your online business.

Direct-mail postcards. Send postcards that contain the offer and a special customer code to existing customers via snail mail. Alert the customer that the code or certificate can be used only once. If you keep track of the customer name or code for each certificate you send, you'll be able to verify when each person uses the certificate.

Physical certificates. Insert actual certificates into packages you ship. Ask customers to mail them back to you for the discount or free product, or use a coding scheme as explained above for electronic redemption of the certificate.

E-mail messages. Make your offer via e-mail and then check the return e-mail address of the person redeeming the certificate to verify his identity. For extra security, include a code number in the e-mail certificate.

Order confirmation forms. When you confirm a customer's order, include a gift certificate for a discount on the next purchase as part of the confirmation notice. Alert customers that they'll have to identify themselves via a customer code or their name in order to receive the discount.

Gift certificates can bring you referral and repeat business in many different ways. The only requirements are your imagination and your business's readiness to deliver value and satisfaction with every sale.

87   SATISFIED CUSTOMERS AND WORD OF MOUTH

Satisfied customers are the mother lode of marketing, the font of referrals, goodwill, and one-to-one promotion of your business. Satisfied customers often buy again, and they also work for you as unpaid members of your marketing team, spreading the good news about your business to friends and relatives. Each satisfied customer you create can potentially bring you a dozen or more new customers.

Most businesses strive for customer satisfaction. The guerrilla difference comes in how you use this priceless resource. Ordinary marketers assume that happy customers will buy again and will tell their friends about their positive experience; guerrilla marketers make sure this happens. Here are four proven ways to convert satisfied customers into repeat buyers and active promoters of your business.

Say thank you. Thank customers for their business at the time of purchase and via a follow-up e-mail letter shortly afterward. Remind them of your undying commitment to customer satisfaction and ask them to refer their friends to you as well. As referred customers buy from you, stay in touch with the original customer by thanking her for the referrals.

Show your appreciation. Happy customers become even happier when they know how much they're appreciated. Show your appreciation by offering special discounts, private sales, or gifts to repeat buyers. Create a preferred customer or frequent buyer club and offer special discounts. This has worked very well for the airlines for decades.

Send a special brochure. Create a special brochure and give it out only to customers. Tailor the brochure's content to promote repeat sales and referrals, and include a discount coupon for future sales or for first-time buyers who are referred by the customer. Include this brochure in the box when you ship merchandise or send it via e-mail following an electronic purchase.

Offer a referral gift. If you offer a large catalog of merchandise, offer a different small item from your catalog as a gift for each new customer referred by an existing customer. A friend of ours in the spicy foods business sends out miniature bottles of Tabasco or samples of other hot sauces in appreciation for new referrals. A mail-order office supplies firm offers a free clock for new customer orders of more than $25.

One positive comment about your business from one friend to another is worth thousands of dollars you might spend in advertising to reach that same person. Find ways to convert your satisfied customers into repeaters and promoters, and you'll be using one of the most powerful weapons at your disposal.

88 TESTIMONIALS

Rather than waiting for customers to spread the word about you, ask them to put their comments in writing and then publish the comments. Quoting real words from real people goes a long way toward establishing your credibility, even when you do it in a paid advertisement or brochure. Testimonials allow new prospects to identify with other people who have been happy with your products or services, which helps them envision themselves using your business.

Testimonials work so well that many companies have built whole advertising campaigns around them. For example, the *Wall Street Journal* has promoted its value to businesses of all kinds by featuring full-page ads that are testimonials from executives in different industries. Along the same line, Apple Computer frequently uses testimonials from business people and celebrities to promote its PowerBook and Macintosh computers and its networking products.

Here are six steps to making testimonials work for you.

Ask for testimonials. The comments you see on many books are there not because the readers happened to pick up the book and then write a note to the publisher, but because the publisher sent the book to the writer and asked for a comment. Most people won't volunteer their written comments about your business even if they're delighted with your service, but they will write a sentence or two if you ask. So ask.

Provide a comment mechanism. Create a handy form that makes it easy for your customers to comment. For example, develop a very brief questionnaire with a few multiple-choice questions followed by a space for comments. If you're doing all you can to satisfy your customers, you'll get more than enough comments to use as ammunition for testimonials. Provide the questionnaire at the point of sale or when a product is delivered, or via a follow-up letter. If you send a follow-up letter, use the opportunity to offer a discount on future purchases as a reward for filling out the questionnaire.

Get details and permission to use them. Anonymous testimonials are almost worthless, because readers know you could easily have made them up. When you ask for comments, get permission to use the comment along with the person's name and company name or home city and state.

Keep comments brief. Use the briefest possible portion of each testimonial to get your point across. That way, you can use more of them from different people in the same amount of screen or paper space.

Select comments for diversity, credibility, and impact. Once you've collected testimonials, the art of using them is choosing the ones that will have the biggest impact on the audience you're trying to reach. Ideally, each of the comments you use will appeal specifically to a certain group of customers because of the words used, the product or service commented on, or the company or city associated with the individual making the comment.

To appeal to the broadest possible audience, use a selection of comments that praise different aspects of your business or different products you sell. Choose comments from an assortment of companies or from people in many different cities, states, or countries.

Use testimonials liberally. As you gather testimonials, include them in a variety of marketing materials. We've seen testimonials on product packages, in brochures, sales letters, catalogs, print and TV ads, on Web sites, and in press releases. Many books include one or several pages of testimonials right inside the cover. You can also collect a group of testimonials into a separate document, title it *What Our Customers Say About Us*, and include it in shipments, press kits, and customer mailings.

Every time you use testimonials, your previous customers are attracting new ones by describing their experience. Positive experiences are a compelling reason for new customers to do business with you.

89 CUSTOMER MAILING LIST

Unless you're selling a product or service that someone is only going to need once, the best source of new business is always the satisfied customers who have bought from you before. A mailing list that gives you access to those customers can provide you with a constant revenue stream. By staying in touch with your customers via e-mail or snail mail, you can tell them about new products or services you're offering, alert them to special events, and generally retain your position in their minds by reminding them that you're still there.

Used wisely, your customer mailing list opens a regular channel of communication between you and your customers. There are many types of documents you can send and many reasons to stay in touch with customers that help promote future sales and foster goodwill. Some of them are:

- Thank-you notes for previous purchases
- Holiday greeting cards
- Birthday cards
- Newsletters or tip sheets about using your products or about topics related to your business (see Chapter 9)
- Gift certificates or coupons for discounts or free merchandise
- Invitations to sales, contests, workshops, seminars, or other special events
- Surveys about customer satisfaction and requests for comments.

You can begin compiling a customer mailing list by collecting names and addresses from your order forms. Add to that all the e-mail addresses of people who ask for your brochure, catalog, or other company information. If you have a storefront, you can also add to your list significantly by asking people to register for mailings. Tell visitors that subscribers to your e-mailing list will be notified every few weeks of upcoming events or significant new features in your store.

To manage your list, use a code that identifies each person as a customer, brochure requester, or list subscriber. That way, you can select different groups and mail tailored documents to each of them.

Treat your mailing list as you would any other essential business tool. Update it regularly, use it frequently, and protect it by making a backup copy and storing it in another location, such as a safe deposit box. The best guerrilla marketers spend 60 percent of their time and energy selling to existing customers. Your mailing list is one of the best ways to do that.

13

Intelligence

NO GUERRILLA WORTH her camouflage goes into battle without a clear and complete understanding of the enemy, the terrain, and any other environmental factors related to the battle. When you market goods or services online, you'll want to know everything you can about the market, your competition, your customers, and the various techniques you can use to do business on the Net. If you don't, you may find yourself attacking the wrong targets at the wrong time with the wrong weapons.

There are two basic types of intelligence guerrillas use: ongoing reports and specific research. For ongoing reports, keep your ear to the ground by reading daily, weekly, and monthly news about your industry and the environment in which you operate. This means regularly scanning newspapers and magazines about business, your industry, and the online marketplace for news and trends.

When you need specific intelligence, there are lots of sources, but knowing how to find them is something else again. Much of what you'll need can be found right online. You use searching, navigation, and other tools of cyberspace to get it. But while online information is there if you know how to find it, off-line sources can deliver information to your desk or doorstep without your having to log on and look for it.

Before we look at specific information weapons, let's look at some methods you can use to find and get hold of information, both online and off.

Web search engines. The Worldwide Web is the most popular portion of the Net, and the most popular method of finding information is using a Worldwide Web search utility, or engine. Just use your Web browser to navigate to the collection of search engines at Netscape's home page (http://www.netscape.com/escapes/internet_search.html), and you can search several parts of cyberspace in different ways. At this one Web address, you'll find several search engines, such as InfoSeek, Lycos, and Webcrawler. Depending on which one you use, you can search the contents of Worldwide Web pages, previous postings to newsgroups, or collections of electronic publications.

A typical search engine looks like this:

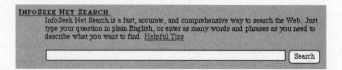

To find information, type in a phrase describing what you want to find and then click the Search button. For example, to get information about business loans, you would type *Business Loans* in the search box. When the search is done, your Web browser will display a list of Web pages containing the phrase you typed along with a link to each page, like this:

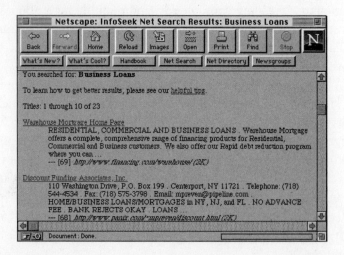

This search found twenty-three different Web pages containing the phrase *Business Loans*. Read the brief descriptions of each page to decide which one you want to look at and then click a link to view a complete page.

Gopher. Gopher is a system linking information servers at hundreds of universities and government agencies around the world.

Information is stored as text documents inside directories on these servers. You need to run a Gopher client program like WinGopher or TurboGopher on your PC to view Gopher servers. When you start up your Gopher client, you're automatically connected to a home Gopher server. The window looks like this:

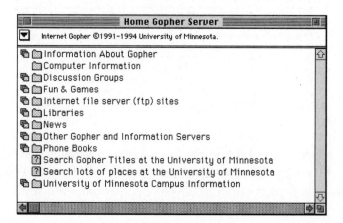

Each collection of information is stored in a directory that looks like a folder here. You can poke through this and other Gopher servers by opening directories and documents. For example, if you opened the *Other Gopher and Information Servers* directory in the window above, you would see a list of other Gopher servers whose menus you could investigate.

To find information more quickly, you can also search for any particular document or directory by name using the Veronica search utility. You access Veronica from right inside your home Gopher server by opening the *Other Gopher and Information Servers* directory and then choosing one of the Veronica search options there. As with a Web search, you use Veronica by typing in a few words from the name of the document or directory you're looking for in a window, like this:

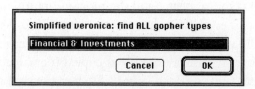

After searching, Veronica presents a window containing all the directories and documents that contain those words in any order, like this:

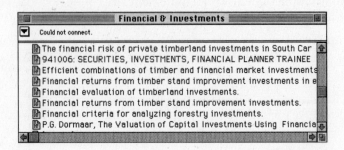

These documents are probably located on several different Gopher servers around the world, but you can open and view any of them by simply double-clicking on them in this window. Veronica lets you limit your search to directory names only or open it up to both document and directory names. However, you can't search for text inside a document.

WAIS. Wide Area Information Servers are collections of documents that you can search for by their contents. For example, if you searched for a phrase you heard from a presidential speech, WAIS would find the document containing the full text of the speech so you could see where and when the speech was given. Typically, you use the Gopher system to navigate to and search the WAIS service.

Ftp and Archie. Ftp, or File Transfer Protocol, is a means of transferring whole files on the Net. Most Internet servers allow Ftp access to their files, but most of the servers at private companies restrict that access to users who have certain passwords. However, university and government servers allow universal (or anonymous) access to their files via Ftp.

To search Ftp servers, you use the programs Archie or Anarchie to display a search window. You then type in keywords contained in the files you want to locate, and the program returns with a list of files whose names contain those words. Unlike the Web, Gopher, and WAIS, however, you don't see the contents of a file when you double-click on it; instead, the file is copied (downloaded) to your own computer, and you open it there. Ftp files can contain graphics, computer programs, and video as well as text. In fact, Ftp is the most common method of distributing free software or graphic files.

Online service search facilities. Every online service has searching facilities you can use to locate specific information databases, discussion groups, and subscriber profiles. If you subscribe to a service like CompuServe, the searching function is a good way to find out if a particular database, such as Hoover's Business Profiles, is available on the service, or to find out if someone you know is also a subscriber.

Magazines and newspapers. Magazines and newspapers are an excellent source of news and in-depth articles about specific topics. You should be reading a major daily newspaper or a daily business newspaper along with monthly magazines or newsletters closely related to your business. Also, arrange to swap magazines with others who subscribe to publications you don't usually see, or to visit your local library and browse through them occasionally, to make sure you're not missing something important. It doesn't take long to skim through a magazine and look for relevant articles. Research like this not only keeps you up to date on current events in your business, it also helps you understand the publicity environment in which you and your competitors do battle.

Libraries. Libraries are the greatest source of information, not because they contain the most information (few of them can match the Net for that) but because they have employees who actually know how to find it. Your Web, Gopher, and Ftp searching savvy will grow with experience, but in the beginning you'll waste some time figuring out just how and where to search. Librarians make a career of knowing how and where to locate specific information on any possible subject.

Intelligence is a key commodity you need to target your attacks and use your weapons well. Most of your competitors ignore this whole aspect of marketing, because they think they're too busy or it's not useful. But every guerrilla understands the importance of intelligence and learns how to tell when she needs information and where to get it when she does.

Now let's look at four weapons you can use in your drive for intelligence.

90 RESEARCH

The Net is a fountain of information, and much of it is research papers, articles, and reports prepared by students, professors, and experts. Right now there are literally billions of pages of facts available in databases, poll results, reports, and articles that you can find through your online connection. Research can help you fine-tune your marketing campaign for specific customers, outrun your competitors, or spot new markets or sales opportunities in other states or countries. Most of the information available on the Net or in libraries is free, but there are also specialized databases, access to which costs you anywhere from a few dollars up to a few hundred dollars a month. Research studies done by consulting firms can cost hundreds or even thousands of dollars. Fee-based information is usually for companies with big pockets, though; guerrillas get most of the same information by investing a little time.

In addition to finding research done by others, you can do your own. Conduct your own surveys or send out questionnaires to find out where your company stands in the recognition or goodwill department or how it stacks up versus its competition.

Here are some specific suggestions for finding and locating the research information you need.

Databases. Databases on online services, WAIS, Gopher, and the Web contain information on market conditions, company financial results, stock prices, international trade policies, opinion poll results, agricultural yields and conditions, consumer buying trends for a variety of products, economic profiles of states or countries, labor statistics, cost-of-living indices, registered patents and trademarks, census and income figures, and many other types of information. The best way to locate databases is to conduct a Web or WAIS search, check your online service's search facility, or get a book that lists online sources of information. Two good ones are *The Internet Yellow Pages*, by Harley Hahn and Rick Stout (Osborne-McGraw, 1994), and *How to Look It Up Online*, by Alfred Glossbrenner (St. Martin's, 1987).

Individual reports or articles. Individual articles or reports on specific topics are available online and off-line. Use a Web search engine, Gopher, or Archie to search the Web, Gopher, and Ftp sites for articles on specific topics. The best way to find them is to try different groups of keywords relating to the topic. Remember, online search utilities will only look for articles whose titles contain the words you specify, and a document's title may have different words from the ones you originally search for. Try different combinations of words if your first search isn't successful.

You'll also learn about research reports relating to your area of business by participating in a discussion group that covers your market. Frequently, authors of such reports post excerpts of them as free samples.

Opinion polls. Online opinion poll results are maintained on Gopher and Web sites by several universities. Use Veronica or a Web search engine to look for polls related to a particular topic. As with a search for articles, you might need to use different groups of keywords to find the poll you're looking for.

Your own surveys. The best way to find out what your customers or prospects want or think is to come right out and ask them. Political candidates, companies, and various government agencies conduct surveys all the time to find out what people think, and you can too. Just explain why you're taking the survey and how you'll use the results, and most people are happy to respond. You can conduct your survey via e-mail, your Web site, or in a discussion group. See *Surveys* on p. 121 for more information.

Big companies pay consultants big bucks to advise them about market conditions and marketing strategies. Most of what these consultants know comes from doing research. Guerrillas save money and get a firsthand picture of battle conditions by conducting their own research. In the online market, you have lots of options. Use them.

91 DISCUSSION GROUP ARCHIVES

Participating in a discussion group is an excellent way to gain visibility, promote goodwill, and build relationships with potential customers. But most discussion groups delete posted comments after a few days or weeks, so you can't tell what was discussed in the past.

Discussion group archives can help you understand a discussion's history. Archives provide intelligence in four ways:

They tell you what people have been talking about. Knowing what people have discussed in the past gives you a broad understanding of a discussion group. This is useful if you're just beginning to participate, because you'll avoid bringing up questions or topics that were covered fairly recently.

They reveal topics of discussion that might be well suited to your marketing purposes. By browsing through a discussion archive, you can look for topics that have come up in the past that would make an ideal context in which to introduce your product or service. People don't always get full and complete answers when they post to a discussion group, and you may be able to supply missing information that didn't come up before. When you find a topic related to your business, e-mail the person who originally posted it and introduce your business.

They indicate what the group is saying about you or your competition. Even if you never participate in a discussion, you can use an archive to find candid comments about your company, products, services, or those of your competition. Comments about your company give you a golden opportunity to contact the author, offering thanks for support or a remedy for his problem. Comments about your competition give you insights about weaknesses you can exploit.

They tell you who is participating in any given discussion. Finally, discussion group archives contain messages posted by people from specific e-mail addresses. It's possible to post a message with a fake address, but few people who are engaged in a serious discussion do that, because they want people to be able to reach them via e-mail. Skim through the archives and add to your database the e-mail addresses of people who are interested in products or services like yours, and then include them in your next promotional mailing.

Not all discussion groups maintain archives, but many do, and savvy guerrillas mine these archives for the information gold they contain. To learn whether or not a discussion group has an archive, post a message on it and ask.

92　SERVER LOGS

If you use a mailbot or host a storefront on the Worldwide Web, your service provider's computer automatically keeps a log of all your visitors or information requesters. The log for a Web site shows only the domain or network name from which each visitor hails, while a mailbot log shows the e-mail address of each person requesting information.

In either case, you can use the server log to gain important insights about who visits your site and then adjust or enhance your marketing attack accordingly. In fact, knowing that the log is available allows you to test various marketing weapons and see the results fairly quickly.

For example, suppose you conduct a conference in a forum on America Online. If the hours and days after that conference show a jump in visitors to your site from aol.com, or a jump in people from aol.com requesting your mailbot document, you can conclude that your conference had promotional value. You may follow your success by using other weapons, such as publishing a newsletter on America Online.

You might also run a series of classified ads that direct people to your Web site or mailbot. Run the ads in different weeks on each of the major online services and then check your server log to see whether there was a corresponding increase in activity from each service's domain during the week your ads ran. This could give you a good idea of how any particular ad is pulling or which service has more ad readers.

Raw visitor, or hit, count information in server logs can also show you if a new directory listing, a link placement campaign, or a publicity salvo creates a jump in visits. The number of hits on a Web page doesn't equal the number of visitors (the ratio is about ten hits for each real visitor), but an increase in the number of hits still indicates an upswing in interest.

To gain more specific visitor information, some Web site operators ask visitors to log in with their e-mail addresses before they can venture freely throughout the site. *Wired* magazine's site (at http://www.wired.com) has done this almost since its inception, and as a result it has very accurate visitor figures on which to base its hefty advertising rates.

If you use a mailbot or Web site, ask your service provider for a weekly or monthly copy of the server log. The log will contain a lot of technical information that isn't important to you, but you can ask your provider to show you how to identify visit counts, visitor domain addresses, dates, and times to extract the marketing-related data from them. Server logs are kept automatically. They're always there waiting for guerrillas with the smarts to use them.

93 MARKETING SAVVY

You can't use marketing savvy if you don't have it, and most people don't. Large corporations and successful startups begin planning and implementing a marketing campaign from day one. In contrast, most small businesses fail or have an extremely rough beginning because they don't put enough effort into marketing. Marketing savvy can smooth your transition from startup to success. Once you understand what marketing is and how to go about it, you're far ahead of most of your competitors. All that remains is the will to do what you know you should do.

You can develop marketing savvy the hard way, by making mistakes and losing money, or you can develop it the easy way, by learning from people with proven track records. Guerrillas conserve energy and finances whenever possible, so in this case the easy path to marketing savvy is also the smart and cost-effective way.

Here are some sources of marketing savvy.

Books. Books like this (and *Guerrilla Marketing Online*) are an excellent place to get a quick transfusion of online marketing savvy. Check out the original *Guerrilla Marketing* if you haven't read it already to gain more insights about how and why guerrillas are different. *Guerrilla Marketing* explains the whole guerrilla approach to marketing and underlies the philosophies in this book. And don't stop there. Scour your bookstore or library for other marketing books. You may not find information that always applies to your situation, but it's better to have too much information on this subject than not enough.

Online discussions. The best online discussion about marketing is the Internet Marketing mailing list. This list has more than five thousand subscribers who do almost nothing but talk about the various methods people are using to market online, what works and what doesn't, and why. You can find out more about this discussion by sending an e-mail message with the subject line *info internet-marketing* to *listproc@popco.com.*

Web sites. Use a Web search engine to search for marketing-related Web sites. Some of them contain valuable tips, articles, and newsletters about online marketing.

Magazines. In addition to your own industry's magazines and a general news or business magazine, read marketing-related issues of *Internet World, Boardwatch,* or *NetGuide* for news about the latest online marketing technologies. Also watch for special issues of magazines like *Sales & Marketing Management, Advertising Age,* and *AdWeek.* At least once every few months, these magazines do a major report on online marketing trends.

Newspapers. A week doesn't go by without a story that has something to do with the Internet in the technology or marketing and media section of the *Wall Street Journal,* and the same goes for *Forbes, Barron's,* and other financial publications. Use these to find out what the big players are doing about online marketing.

The more you know about marketing, the better prepared you are to do battle. Marketing savvy helps you choose your weapons more effectively and aim them with deadly accuracy. By absorbing as much marketing savvy as possible, you'll learn that in some way, everything you do is marketing, and that's the most important guerrilla knowledge of all.

14

Guerrilla Attitudes

THROUGHOUT THIS BOOK, we've laid out an array of weapons you can use to succeed in the online marketplace. But none of the other weapons are as important as the seven in this chapter. Without guerrilla attitudes, you can't use any of the other weapons to their best advantage.

Some people are born with the soul of a guerrilla: they're naturally competitive, confident, imaginative, and enthusiastic. Others come to learn the importance of these traits and work hard to acquire them. Many people never understand or use these weapons at all. Guerrillas succeed because they believe from the bottom of their hearts that they deserve to succeed, and they don't let anything stop them. They use every means at their disposal to win.

Guerrilla attitudes are the backbone of your marketing program, but they're not easy to maintain. You can psyche yourself up to embrace any of the weapons in this chapter for a few hours or a few days, but it's hard to keep using them day in and day out. The enthusiasm you begin with on a Monday morning can fade by lunchtime. Corporations that spend thousands on motivational training classes for their employees often see a surge of enthusiasm immediately following the training, only to find things drifting back to the same old routine after a week or two.

But the best marketing programs work all day, every day, and your guerrilla attitudes must too. You may add or change weapons during your marketing program, but true guerrillas spend a lot of their energy each day *using* marketing weapons, and attitudes are always at the top of the list. And attitudes pay: your drive, imagination, and enthusiasm will help you win even when your competitors are much larger and better financed.

As you come to understand the importance of guerrilla attitudes, teach them to your employees and help them maintain them. Hold daily or weekly meetings that focus on attitudes and demonstrate them in all your dealings with your staff. Your positive attitudes will rub off on your employees, and from there onto your customers, and from there onto your bottom line.

Few of your competitors recognize or use the weapons in this chapter, so you'll gain a huge advantage by using any of them at all. But all of the weapons in this chapter are absolutely free, so you should begin using them all as soon as possible.

94 ENTHUSIASM

Enthusiasm is highly contagious. It creates an atmosphere of excitement and fun surrounding whatever you do. Your employees and customers are swept up in that atmosphere. When you're excited about your products, your employees are excited about them too, and that always means more sales.

In a physical store, enthusiasm in the air makes for happier customers. Upbeat salespeople who love what they sell naturally infect customers with a desire to buy. Your customers won't physically meet you or your employees in your online business, but you can still convey enthusiasm in several ways:

- Faster and especially courteous responses to orders or questions
- A lively storefront design
- Compelling and evocative brochures, articles, and storefront copy.

When a Web site is designed by enthusiastic people, it shows in the text and in the graphics. The site has its own unique personality rather than simply being a collection of text about yet another product or service. Some examples of this on the Web are the Ragu site (http://www.eat.com), the Rolling Stones site (http://www.stones.com), and the *Wired* magazine site (http://www.wired.com). And even if you're doing business from an e-mail box, a rapid response to orders or e-mail always shows that you're ready and willing to do business.

But you can't manufacture enthusiasm out of thin air. It's not just a matter of sprinkling capital letters, asterisks, boldface type, or exclamation points throughout your text. It's a feeling you and your employees have when serving your customers, processing orders, participating in online discussions, or creating your company's online information. You can't fake enthusiasm, either. It's either a genuine emotion or it falls flat.

Here are some ways to create and maintain enthusiasm.

Daily or weekly meetings. Enthusiasm runs in cycles. Monday mornings are often times of high enthusiasm, but it ebbs as the day or week wears on. Hold daily meetings just after lunch to pump up the excitement level, or schedule a meeting at mid-week to arrest the downward spiral of enthusiasm and reverse its course. Make meetings spontaneous and hold them at different times so they don't become part of the routine.

New product, feature, or benefit bulletins. When you take on new products, offer a special promotion, or discover new benefits for a product or service, issue a bulletin and make sure your whole staff gets it at once. Call an impromptu meeting to explain the change. Any new reason for excitement should be announced to everyone immediately.

Sales contests. Hold sales contests to give staffers something to shoot for.

Comment sessions. Give people at every level of your company a voice in decisions related to marketing, advertising, and sales. People are naturally more enthusiastic about and committed to a process when they have something to do with its management.

Employee appreciation. Silicon Valley companies hold weekly beer busts, off-site retreats, and lavish Christmas parties to make their employees feel good about working for them. Do what you can to make your employees happy. When they like your company, they're more enthusiastic about their work.

Presentations by product designers or creators. Nobody is as enthusiastic about a product as the person who created it, yet few marketers think to schedule presentations by those people as a means of motivating their staff. By the time we hear about most products we sell, the originator's enthusiasm has been diluted through a succession of copywriters, sales managers, and others in the distribution or information chain. But when your staff sees a presentation from the father or mother of a product, the excitement rubs off. You'll get better Web page designs for that product and better service from the staffers who process orders for or answer questions about it.

For example, when Harvey Mackay began promoting *How to Swim with the Sharks Without Being Eaten Alive,* he realized that customers (bookstores in this case) wouldn't be excited about his book unless the people selling it were excited about it. He gave in-person presentations to the salespeople at his publishing house and his book distributors. The salespeople contracted Harvey's enthusiasm, and the result was a *New York Times* bestseller.

Use some of these proven ways to generate and maintain enthusiasm, and your company will be a happier place to work and to buy from.

95 CONFIDENCE

Confidence is an unshakable belief in yourself, your company, and your products. This is a particularly important weapon in cyberspace, because so many of the people shopping online are nervous about the technology and the vendors using it to sell. Customers can't see and talk to actual human beings on the Net, but if you exude confidence, your customers will feel confident too. Your confidence makes them more comfortable, so it makes your company easier to buy from than your competitors.

If enthusiasm is a trait you infect others with, confidence is one that must be earned. And you can't begin to earn it from others if you don't have it yourself. If you're not completely confident of the value of the products or services you sell, you're in the wrong business.

But having confidence yourself and earning it from others are two different things. You earn confidence through your manner and through specific actions. Here are four key traits you need to earn confidence.

Honesty. Dishonesty is fine if nobody knows you're being dishonest — and if you can stand the moral implications. The trouble is that your employees *will* know you're being dishonest, and their attitudes will reflect that knowledge. When you're honest, you can have complete confidence in everything you say, because it's the truth. Deal honestly with your employees and customers, and their confidence in you will go nowhere but up.

Integrity. When you have integrity, people can rely on you absolutely to treat them fairly and make good on your promises, no matter what the cost. When you treat your employees this way and urge them to treat customers the same way, it shows. You eliminate dissatisfaction and enhance your reputation.

Responsibility. This is your willingness to say "The buck stops here" for every aspect of your business. Being responsible means you're willing and able to respond quickly, whether the problem is a disgruntled employee or an unhappy customer.

Consistency. Consistency is partially achieved through honesty, but other factors are involved. Through careful planning, you should arrive at business and marketing plans that will serve you well for months or years. Once you've made your plans, stick with them. When you change direction every few weeks, people lose confidence in your business acumen and your ability to lead.

To spread confidence from yourself to your customers and employees, make your intentions about all these traits well known to them. Write a fairness statement in your employee handbook, on your walls, and in your catalogs and brochures. In addition to these traits, take these three specific actions to inspire confidence:

- Offer an unconditional guarantee on everything you sell.
- Distribute free samples or give demonstrations of your products.
- Become an expert in the use of your products and share that expertise with everyone who asks for it.

Once you've adopted these traits and undertaken these actions, you've paved the way for complete confidence among your employees and customers. This firm foundation of confidence will anchor your reputation and serve you well through any temporary ups and downs.

96 REALISTIC EXPECTATIONS

Like any new marketing channel, the online marketplace is the great hope of failed business people everywhere. They read hyped-up reports about the cyberspace explosion in a newspaper and think that here at last is a medium that will save their business from certain doom. Thousands of would-be millionaires have jumped onto the Net in hopes of spinning technology into gold. But the Net is a communications medium, no more. It's not a magic profit machine, any more than any other medium is.

When you open your online business, do it with realistic expectations. If your expectations are grounded in reality, you'll know you need to put the necessary effort into marketing. If you expect the Net to do your marketing for you, you'll be sadly disappointed. People who think the Net is an automatic gold mine sit back and wait for profits to roll in. And while they're sitting and waiting, guerrillas who know what to expect do what it takes to make the Net pay.

Here's how to develop and live by a set of realistic expectations on the Net.

Conduct diligent research. Cyberspace won't turn a bad business idea into a good one, and it won't chase your competitors away. Before venturing into the online marketplace, conduct diligent research about the feasibility of your business idea and the odds of your being able to sell it online. The Net just isn't suited for every business on the planet. For example, putting your local rug cleaning business or muffler shop online probably won't increase your business. Your business purpose must be matched to the realities of online marketing and sales.

There are four key questions you should ask yourself before going online.

1. *Can I reach my customers effectively online?* If your customers aren't online or willing to go online, it makes no sense to be there.
2. *Does my business success rely on the uniqueness of my offering, and if so, is my idea better than or different from those of any competitors?* If your business idea seems to have been tried by a lot of other companies, seek a niche within the broader market for those goods or services. (See *Product/service niche* in Chapter 1.)
3. *Can I add value, service, convenience, or other attributes to my off-line business by going online?* An online catalog can be updated daily or weekly at very low cost, for example, and it gives people who may not see your printed catalog access to your merchandise.
4. *Do I understand the online market well enough to answer the previous questions intelligently?* If you haven't done enough ba-

sic reading and exploration of the online market, you can't possibly understand what is or isn't possible there. Spend some time learning about the online world before you answer the other questions.

If you can confidently answer "yes" to these questions, you probably have a solid idea for the online marketplace. But you'll have to explore that marketplace and do some diligent research to find out. (For more on research, see p. 158 in Chapter 13.)

Make a business plan. If you're convinced your idea is good, make a detailed business plan that identifies your specific market, your customers, your competition, and your projected income and expenses for at least the first year. Don't assume the money will roll in from day one, either. Early online marketers made wildly optimistic projections about sales and profits based on the total number of people thought to be online, but not all cybernauts are potential customers. In fact, the most reliable study to date, by the A. C. Neilsen Company, shows that only 14 percent of cybernauts actually buy things online. Set conservative goals for your first year in business. In this case, a little pessimism is good: you won't be disappointed if sales are as low as you project, and you'll be pleasantly surprised if they're better.

Update your information constantly. Initial research sets your initial expectations. Further research helps you maintain the reality of your outlook indefinitely. Changes in your competition, marketing technology, and online populations can all affect your expectations and projections.

Most businesses fail because of unrealistic expectations. People often underestimate the cost of establishing a business, the market for their products or services, or the strength of the competition. Guerrillas survey every battlefield completely before committing themselves, and they never choose a fight they can't win.

97 CURIOSITY

Curiosity is like fresh air. A continuous search for new ideas keeps your marketing campaign fresh, yourself and your employees enthusiastic about doing business, and your customers interested. Curiosity leads to your offering new products or services. It drives you to explore new marketing techniques and to learn more about what your customers really want.

When you begin planning your online campaign, you're intensely curious about the hows and whys of online commerce. But as the weeks and months wear on and you get caught up in the day-to-day operations of your business, it can be hard to maintain your curiosity level. You can't afford to let it lapse, though, because when it does, your business stagnates and your customers go elsewhere. This is more true online than anywhere else. Cybernauts demand new and interesting things all the time, so your long-term survival depends on your curiosity and the new ideas it generates.

Here are three ways to stimulate and maintain curiosity.

Read print magazines and newsletters. A steady diet of magazines and newsletters about the online marketplace will help maintain your interest and curiosity, because these magazines constantly report on the newest developments. You gather new information every time you go online, but the fact is that you spend most of your time off-line. Print publications are portable and easy to scan for important facts.

Explore cyberspace. Keep in mind, though, that magazines are a month or two behind the present time, so cyberspace is always the most current source of information. Set aside an hour or two each week just to cruise around the Net to see what's out there. Use the time to follow up on resources mentioned in discussion groups or to browse in the mega-directories like Yahoo and explore Web sites by pointing and clicking. Try new technologies, such as demonstrations of new sound, video, or virtual reality products.

Ask for suggestions. Ask for and reward people for suggestions or comments about your business. Many companies reward employees who make good suggestions about cost savings, new products, or marketing, and you should do the same. Some of the most successful products have come from employee ideas. For example, the Post-It note started out as something 3M employees used among themselves.

It's fatal to assume that you know more about what your customers want than they do. Microsoft relies heavily on suggestions from customers when it makes new versions of its products. Chrysler's latest minivans incorporate hundreds of changes suggested by customers. When you get a good suggestion, implement it, thank the person for it, and make it known in public who suggested it. You'll forge an almost unbreakable bond with that person.

Another reason to thank people for suggestions is the publicity you may create in the process. For example, awarding the first samples of a new or improved product to people who suggested changes is a good lead-in for a press release about the product itself.

But even if you don't publicly reward people for suggestions, the process of asking for them gives customers and employees a larger stake in your company's success. People who have input into how your company develops will become frequent visitors and tireless promoters of your business.

Curiosity is the sign of a lively mind. Guerrillas are constantly searching for new ways to blow away the competition, and curiosity is the engine that drives them.

98 IMAGINATION

In just a few short years, the online world has evolved from an explosion of new technologies to a collection of Web sites that frequently look very much the same. Imagination is the weapon you use to make your storefront or business stand out from the others.

It's easy to spot the online stores with little or no imagination behind them. They're faithful (and often ineffective) electronic re-creations of off-line catalogs and brochures. The imaginative storefronts, in contrast, leverage the capabilities of cyberspace to provide a shopping experience that can't be had in the off-line world. Some traits of an imaginative storefront are:

- interaction among shoppers via chat rooms or message boards
- real-time conferences with experts
- true hypertext capabilities that reveal several levels of information at the viewer's discretion
- 3-D (or virtual reality) renderings of objects and spaces
- video or sound clips.

Most people are born with good imaginations, but in the crush of schooling, conducting business, and living day-to-day life, we forget just how potent our imaginations can be. And many of us never know how profitable they can be. The following tips will help stimulate your imagination and your profits.

Read. We've mentioned reading research, magazines, newspapers, and online sources of information, but by reading in this case we mean other things. Read biographies, novels, and nonfiction books about various topics. Reading is calisthenics for the mind, and it always stimulates imagination. It could well be that reading the latest Michael Crichton book will give you an idea that makes a huge difference in your business.

Get out of the office. Routine murders imagination and creativity. Shake up your routine once in a while by taking walks or just going for a drive. Some people get their best ideas while jogging, fishing, sailing, or taking a shower.

Take notes. When you get a new idea, write it down or sketch it out. Otherwise, it's nothing more than a thought bubble that surfaces, pops, and disappears. One friend of ours leaves notepads and pencils in every room of his house so he's never far from them when an idea strikes. Other people carry a pocket notebook just for jotting down ideas.

Talk about new ideas. Having an idea and writing it down are only the beginning. You can continue the creative process by discussing your thoughts with others. In her book *The Popcorn Report*, marketing consultant Faith Popcorn writes at length about the importance of having a group of people with whom you can kick around ideas. She calls her group a Brain Reserve. Your discussion partners can be friends, neighbors, or colleagues, but brainpower and creativity are what you seek, not status. It could be that your dentist is a better sounding board for new product ideas than your marketing director.

Test new ideas. When you've kicked an idea around and reached agreement that it's a good one, test it. Come up with a way to build a prototype, test a new ad campaign, or try a new motivational program with your employees. By testing small sample groups you'll quickly prove or disprove the idea's validity. It's better to test an idea and see it fail than to spend your life wondering if it would have made a difference.

Imagination keeps your business fresh. Keeping your nose to the grindstone is fine if you have problems with self-discipline, but guerrillas are hard workers anyway. Once your business is running smoothly, have the faith to delegate the day-to-day work to trusted employees. While your competitors are focusing on the grindstone, you should be constantly working on new ideas to make your business better.

99   OBJECTIVITY

Subjective judgments have been responsible for some of the biggest marketing flops in history. Recall New Coke, the Edsel, and clear whiskey, to name just three. What seems like a terrific idea on the drawing board sometimes dies when you present it to the customers you're hoping to attract. Still, many companies never bother to ask the basic question *Do our customers want this?*

Once you get into a subjective mindset, you're on a dangerous path toward customer dissatisfaction. Rather than wondering what you can add to attract customers, you sit and congratulate yourself on a brilliant idea and then puzzle over why it doesn't sell.

The best marketers are those who are best able to put themselves right inside the customer's mind. Here are four ways to do that.

Pretend you're the customer. Act like a customer on a regular basis to stay in touch with the online shopping experience. Buy things online yourself. Visit your own storefront and try to be objective about what you see there and how it might be improved. Send in an order via your own storefront to see how it's processed — use a different name and have the order sent to a friend, if necessary.

Listen to your customers. Talk to your customers whenever possible, either on the phone or via e-mail. Ask them how you're doing and how you can do better. Send out questionnaires and offer a small gift for returning it. Take customers to lunch and talk about them, not you. This not only increases your understanding of customer needs, it improves goodwill at the same time.

Listen to your staff. Talk regularly with your employees about their experiences with your procedures and policies and with customers they serve. Some of your best customers will often tell an employee something they wouldn't tell you, especially if the employee is a friend. Employees also know their jobs better than you do and frequently have better ideas about how to improve them.

Travel. It's hard to think objectively about what other people might want or need when you're never exposed to other people. Consumers in Michigan or Minnesota sometimes have different needs from those in Mississippi or Alabama. Travel to other cities or countries and talk with the people there. Listen to what they're telling you. You may discover a new market in another city or recognize an unfilled need that's common throughout the world.

Objectivity allows you to think more clearly about new products or services. It's also the fastest way to improve customer and employee relations. You can't begin treating people the way they would like to be treated unless you know how they would like to be treated. When you strive for objectivity, you're really striving to understand and care about serving the needs of others. No successful business was ever built without meeting that fundamental goal.

100 COMPETITIVENESS

And so we come to the last and single most important weapon in this book. Great ideas, good intentions, money, and plans are nothing without a strong drive to compete. True guerrillas are willing to sacrifice everything in order to win. And that doesn't mean lying, cheating, or stealing, because in guerrilla terms, that's not winning.

For a guerrilla, winning is:

- making a profit by delivering value in products or services and building lasting customer relationships;
- rising above your competition through a superior reputation, higher sales, or greater market share; and
- making yourself happy in the process.

Some guerrillas have one-person companies and others run billion-dollar enterprises, but they all believe completely in the rightness of what they're doing, and they're all fulfilled by it.

When you're competitive, you have a desire to win on these terms. Being competitive means several things:

Winning through as many means possible. We've described one hundred weapons in this book. Being competitive is using as many of them as you can. If you're not using at least fifty or sixty of them, you're not a guerrilla. In fact, the most successful guerrillas are always trying to incorporate more weapons; for example, the president of a nationally known diet program recently attended a Guerrilla Marketing workshop because he was only using about eighty weapons and wanted to figure out how to use the rest of them. And the list doesn't stop with the weapons in this book: you'll discover new ones of your own as you continue on the guerrilla path.

Constantly striving to do better. Weapons rust from disuse, and it's not enough to decide you're going to use a weapon, spend a little time with it, and then drop it. Marketing is a full-time job, and you must use your weapons continuously, or you might as well not use them at all.

Remaining aware of the competitive environment. Companies with great products have often seen their fortunes wane because they failed to understand the competitive environment. For example, Apple Computer was years ahead of Microsoft Windows with its Macintosh computer. By licensing its software and pricing its machines competitively, Apple could have taken a controlling share of the personal computer market. By focusing on short-term profit margins instead, the company relegated itself to a niche.

Respecting your competitors, not knocking them. Guerrillas honor their competitors, because they're not afraid of them. The way to your customers' hearts is to honor your competition and rise above it.

Having a sincere desire to be of service. Guerrillas are a positive force in their communities and in their markets. They do right by their employees and customers because they want to. They do right because it's fun, satisfying, and adds to the monetary rewards of a successful business.

Recognizing that marketing isn't *part* of a guerrilla's job, it *is* a guerrilla's job. Everything you do has a marketing component, whether it's getting together with friends or planning a new advertising campaign. Business guides recommend that you spend at least 50 percent of your time doing specific marketing functions to bring in new business. But guerrillas realize that all their actions affect their reputation, visibility, goodwill, and customer satisfaction in some way, whether they're at work or not. Become a walking demonstration of your honesty, professionalism, and integrity in everything you do, and you'll be a guerrilla.

When you're a true guerrilla, you believe in all these aspects of winning and competitiveness. You practice them day in and day out and find creative solutions to obstacles you encounter along the way. Guerrillas don't quit and they don't complain, because every day brings new opportunities for fulfillment.

Great monetary and personal rewards are out there for anyone with the guts and determination to go after them. Guerrillas reap these rewards every day. You now have the tools to get them yourself.

Glossary

This glossary will help you understand the meanings of technical words used throughout the book. When a definition here contains a word in italics, that word is defined elsewhere.

address book — A personal directory of *e-mail* addresses stored and maintained with one's e-mail program.

alias — A collection of *e-mail* addresses stored under one name to facilitate addressing mail to a particular group of users.

Archie — A search utility that surveys all *Ftp* sites once a month and builds an index of all software at those sites. The index is stored on an Archie *server* on the *Net*. Short for "archiver," it was written by Peter Deutsch and Alan Emtage at McGill University in Canada in 1990. There are dozens of Archie servers worldwide.

browser — A program used to access and view information on *Worldwide Web, Gopher,* or *WAIS servers.*

Bulletin board system (BBS) — Any computer system and software with one or more telephone lines that will accept a phone call from another computer at any time with little or no prior arrangement for access.

chat room — An area in an *online service* or *BBS* where several users can meet simultaneously and exchange typed messages.

conference — A large *chat* session that features a main speaker and an audience that asks questions.

cybernaut — One who uses the *Internet.*

cyberspace — Another name for the online universe.

directory — A named subsection of the storage space on a *server* or computer storage disk.

discussion group — An electronic message board on an *online service, BBS,* or the *Net* that contains messages focusing on a specific topic.

domain — A category of *network* on the *Internet,* or a specific network name, called a *domain name.* Every Internet address has a suffix that indicates its domain. Some common domain suffixes are .com (commercial organizations), .edu (education), .gov (government), and .net (network).

domain name service — A service offered by an *ISP* which registers customers' servers as distinct *Internet domains.*

download — To retrieve a file from an *online service, BBS,* or *Internet server.*

electronic mail (e-mail) — A means of exchanging typed messages between computer users in which messages are sent to specific addresses and stored in mailboxes.

FAQs (Frequently Asked Questions) — A collection of frequent questions about a particular discussion group, bulletin board, *SIG, Internet* service, or other subject.

flame — *v.* To send a poison-pen *e-mail* letter to another *Internet* user, usually someone who has violated *netiquette. n.* A poison-pen *e-mail* letter.

forum — The name used for a *discussion group* on an *online service* or *BBS.*

From box — The space at the top of an *e-mail* message that indicates who the message is from.

Ftp (File transfer protocol) — A program that allows you to transfer files to and from other computers on the *Internet.*

Gopher — A method of locating information on the *Internet.* Also a type of server that uses that location method and a software program used to locate such servers. Created in 1991 at the University of Minnesota, Gopher was the first easy-to-use Internet searching and browsing system.

header — The portion of an *e-mail* document that contains the mailing address (or To address), the return address (or From address), and subject information.

hit — A specific access of a *server* by a user. Server traffic is sometimes measured in hits per hour or hits per day. An active Net server has thousands of hits per day. That is, it is accessed thousands of times per day by various users.

home page — The introductory or menu page of a *Web site.* A home page usually contains the site's name and a directory of its contents.

HTML (Hypertext markup language) — The programming language used to store and present information on *Worldwide Web servers*.

HTTP (Hypertext Transfer Protocol) — The communications protocol, or set of technical rules, through which *Worldwide Web* information is linked on the *Internet*.

hypertext link — An automatic link on the *Worldwide Web* that connects a word, phrase, or picture on one *server* with another server. When a user selects a linked phrase or picture, that user is automatically connected to the server to which it is linked.

image map — A graphic image on the Worldwide Web that contains several *hypertext links*, each of which is located in a different part of the image.

Internet — An international data communications pathway that links thousands of computer *networks* together. Also called the Net.

Internet service provider (ISP) — A company or organization that offers *Internet* access to customers for a fee. Also called an IAP, or Internet access provider.

lurker — Someone who monitors a *mailing list, forum,* or *newsgroup* without *posting* to it.

mailbot — A program that responds automatically to incoming *e-mail*. A mailbot receives e-mail messages and then replies to them automatically by sending messages or files to their authors.

mailing list — An electronic discussion carried out with *e-mail* messages rather than with an electronic message board. Rather than *posting* a message to a discussion board, you send it to a mailing list's e-mail address. All subscribers to a mailing list receive copies of all messages sent to that list's address.

mailing list manager — A program that collects and distributes *e-mail* messages to a mailing list.

modem — A device that allows a computer to connect with other computers over standard telephone lines by dialing phone numbers.

Mosaic — A *Worldwide Web browser* program.

navigator — A *browser* used to search for and display information on the *Internet*.

Net — Shorthand for *Internet*.

netiquette — Rules of conduct for *Internet* users.

netizen — Someone who uses the *Internet*; a member of the Internet community of users.

Netscape — A *Worldwide Web browser* program, and the name of the company that makes it.

newbie — A newcomer to the *Internet* or to an *online service*.

newsgroup — A message board on the Internet that focuses on a particular subject. Also known as a *Usenet* newsgroup.

newsreader — A program that allows you to read *newsgroups* on the *Internet*.

online service — A large commercial bulletin board system that accommodates hundreds or thousands of users at once, offers a wide variety of services and information, and charges a monthly subscription fee.

post — *v.* To send a message to a discussion group or mailing list. *n.* A message posted to a *discussion group* or sent to a *mailing list*.

server — A computer that stores files and makes them available to other users on a network or on the Internet.

server log — A record of users accessing a particular *server*.

signature — A block of information used to sign the end of an *e-mail* or *discussion group* message. It usually includes an author name, company name, e-mail address, and other information.

site — A distinct location for information on the Internet.

snail mail — A *cybernaut's* term for paper or postal mail.

spam — To cross-post or mass-mail unsolicited electronic messages to a large number of *discussion groups* or individuals on the Net.

special interest group (SIG) — Another name for a forum or discussion group. Often used on CompuServe.

storefront — A fixed location on the *Worldwide Web*, an *online service*, or a *bulletin board system* that stores a collection of information about your business which can be accessed by others at any time.

T1, T2, T3, and T4 lines — High-speed telephone lines that are leased from a telephone company and provide an ongoing connection for data transfers.

Telnet — A program that allows you to log on to other computers or bulletin board systems on the Internet and run programs on them remotely.

Thread — A group of *newsgroup* messages on the same topic, often a sequence of replies and comments about an initial message.

top menu — The menu on a *server* that functions as its table of contents.

Unix — A powerful computer operating system that is used on many *Internet servers*.

upload — To transfer a file from your PC to a *BBS, online service,* or a *server* on the *Net*.

URL (Universal Resource Locator) — A standardized address format used for *Internet* addresses, especially for Worldwide Web addresses.

Usenet — The largest collection of *newsgroups* on the Internet.

Veronica — A program that locates information stored on *Gopher servers*. The name is an acronym for Very Easy Rodent-Oriented Net-wide Index to Computerized Archives.

WAIS (Wide Area Information Servers) — A system for searching for files or programs via groups of keywords. Also, *servers* that are set up to be accessed by that system.

Web — Shorthand for *Worldwide Web*.

Web site — A *storefront* located on the *Web*.

Worldwide Web — A collection of information located on many Internet *servers*, which can be accessed with a *browser* or by navigating via *hypertext links*.

'zine — An electronic publication on one very specific topic, published by one person or a handful of people and distributed at intervals for free over the *Internet*.

**You can continue to be a guerrilla with
The Guerrilla Marketing Newsletter!**

The Guerrilla Marketing Newsletter provides you with state-of-the-moment insights to maximize the profits you will obtain through marketing. The newsletter has been created to furnish you with the cream of the new guerrilla marketing information from around the world. It is filled with practical advice, the latest research, upcoming trends, and brand-new marketing techniques — all designed to pay off your bottom line.

A yearly subscription costs $49 for six issues.

All subscribers to *The Guerrilla Marketing Newsletter* are given this unique and powerful guarantee: If you aren't convinced after examining your first issue for 30 days that the newsletter will raise your profits, your subscription fee will be refunded — along with $2 just for trying.

To subscribe, merely call or write:

> Guerrilla Marketing International
> 260 Cascade Drive, P.O. Box 1336
> Mill Valley, CA 94942, U.S.A.
> 1-800-748-6444
> In California, 415-381-8361

Get the Complete Guerrilla Arsenal!

Guerrilla Marketing: Secrets for Making Big Profits from Your Small Business   ISBN 0-395-64496-8 $11.95

The book that started the Guerrilla Marketing revolution, now completely revised and updated for the nineties. Full of the latest strategies, information on the latest technologies, new programs for targeted prospects, and management lessons for the twenty-first century.

Guerrilla Financing: Alternative Techniques to Finance Any Small Business   ISBN 0-395-52264-1 $10.95

The ultimate sourcebook for finance in the 1990s, and the first book to describe in detail all the traditional and alternative sources of funding for small and medium-size businesses.

Guerrilla Marketing Attack: New Strategies, Tactics, and Weapons for Winning Big Profits   ISBN 0-395-50220-9 $9.95

A companion to *Guerrilla Marketing*, this book arms small and medium-size business with vital information about direct marketing, customer relations, cable TV, desktop publishing, ZIP code inserts, TV shopping networks, and much more.

Guerrilla Marketing Excellence: The Fifty Golden Rules for Small-Business Success   ISBN 0-395-60844-9 $9.95

Jay Levinson delivers the 50 basic truths of guerrilla marketing that can make or break your company, including the crucial difference between profits and sales, marketing in a recession, and the latest uses of video and television to assure distribution.

Guerrilla Selling: Unconventional Weapons and Tactics for Increasing Your Sales   ISBN 0-395-57820-5 $9.95

Today's increasingly competitive business environment requires new skills and commitment from salespeople. Guerrilla Selling presents unconventional selling tactics that are essential for success.

The Guerrilla Marketing Handbook   ISBN 0-395-70013-2 $14.95

The Guerrilla Marketing Handbook presents Jay Levinson's entire arsenal of marketing weaponry, including a step-by-step guide to developing a marketing campaign and detailed descriptions of over 100 marketing tools.

Guerrilla Advertising: Cost-Effective Tactics for Small-Business Success   ISBN 0-395-68718-9 $11.95

Jay Levinson applies his proven guerrilla philosophy to advertising. Teeming with anecdotes about past and current advertising successes and failures, the book entertains as it teaches the nuts and bolts of advertising for small businesses.

Guerrilla Marketing Online   ISBN 0-395-72859-2 $12.95

From getting acquainted with Internet culture to creating a complete online marketing plan, *Guerrilla Marketing Online* is the basic training entrepreneurs need to take Jay Levinson's proven marketing tactics to the new and important marketplace of the Internet.

These titles are available through bookstores, or you can order directly from Houghton Mifflin at 1-800-225-3362.